MW01711559

MEXICAN SUMMER AND OTHER SEASONS

By David T. Snyder

Kleenan Press

31117 Country Bluff

Farmington Hills, Michigan 48331-1009

Telephone or Fax: 248/661-0543

Library of Congress Control Number 2002117382

Printed in the United States of America

ISBN 0-9745081-0-1

For Annie -

who knows my virtues
and faults
better than anyone

Author's Note

This book is my final testament to a mainly ordinary life lived through most of the 20th Century. It's a combination of personal recollection and historical allusion with real events and personalities sometimes disguised to avoid the embarrassment most of them don't deserve.

The historical material is superficial and is intended only to provide a broad backdrop to the more parochial, but nevertheless central, elements of the narrative. There's a lot of smoking and drinking - mainly hard liquor and beer, not wine - in this book, but that's the way things were in some circles before modernity set in.

I could describe the effort as a semi-fictional memoir with historical overtones, but I won't. It's simply an attempt to use personal anecdotal material and history to reveal something about a short period in the long span of recorded time. I don't mean to imply that the 20th Century's mid-point was special compared with other periods, but it was - as all periods are - unique.

I wrote this book for my own private reasons and not with any expectation it would interest anyone else. I just wanted to give my rather long life some perspective and this is the way I chose to do it. If you read the thing, I trust it won't bore you beyond endurance. Up to endurance, perhaps, but not beyond.

Dave Snyder

Farmington Hills, Michigan

October 2002

ONE

I spent a summer in Mexico so long ago it sometimes seems like something from someone else's life. But so many memories from those few fleeting months linger - crowding out other, perhaps more important, things I've experienced - that I've come to realize it was a time of extraordinary personal importance to me.

For reasons I'll explain, I went to Taxco, an old mining town turned tourist refuge in the mountains about half way between Mexico City to the north and Acapulco to the south on the Pacific coast. It was very early summer in 1950, only days before the North Koreans in an act of blatant nastiness sent seven infantry divisions and some armor - more than 90,000 troops - across the frontier into South Korea. It was also not long before my friend, Gregory Upp, was killed on a rural Missouri highway. The two incidents are obviously unrelated, except that both are for me inextricably and permanently associated with that summer in Mexico.

I was scarcely aware of the Korean War during its early months only a couple of years after my own discharge from the Marine Corps, and I didn't learn of Greg's death until my return to the United States at summer's end. Communication across international boundaries in those days, even with contiguous Mexico, was not nearly as prompt as it was to become later in the century.

Greg had recently graduated from the University of Missouri at Columbia and had been accepted for graduate work in Anthropology at Northwestern near Chicago. He was on a summer-long archeological "dig" when he inadvertently put his skinny body in the path of a car traveling at highway speed on a dark road. He had gone to fetch beer.

The dark road was a stretch of old U.S. 40 near Mineola, Missouri, less by a good deal than a metropolis and the nearest community to a place where Greg and other like-minded souls were rummaging through Indian mounds for who-knows-what. Then, white men could disinter Native American remains, both physical and cultural, with impunity, providing they didn't damage to any significant extent the local agricultural crops. It was a great time to be an archeologist in America.

In Columbia as an undergraduate, Greg often sat at the bar in the old Stein Club, one of the student hang-outs, and sorted arrowheads as he drank beer. He refused; however, to call them arrowheads, insisting they were "projectile points" and that "only some unlearned fool would call a projectile point an arrowhead." One man's projectile point is another man's rock, the bartender, an engineering student, once told him, adding that Greg's old shoe box full of dusty stone did little to promote a scientific image. Greg ignored the slur and continued to sip his beer and sort projectile points. We kidded him for some time about projectile points and only stopped when we discovered the words had surreptitiously crept into our own vocabularies. It's now more than 50 years later and I'm reluctant to call a projectile point an arrowhead.

I met Greg at our St. Louis high school through a mutual friend, Jerry Metcalf, who with three other friends enlisted in the Marine Corps with me in the late summer of 1946 after our graduations in June. We had barely missed military service in the second world war and were a bitterly disappointed group of 17-year-olds, an attitude that would eventually be replaced with an enduring awareness of how lucky we really were. It doesn't take genius to know that war is not only dangerous but a mainly nonproductive and in most cases a scarcely entertaining enterprise. We came a little late to that awareness, but we got there.

Greg was a budding intellectual — a description I don't particularly like and one he would have hated - but he disguised that tendency with a genuine interest in sports, particularly baseball, an overtly horny disposition and smutty talk. At a time when public expletives were really deleted, he used a lot of public expletives that were not only an affront to public decency but an embarrassment to his friends. We used the same language among ourselves, but not around adults and especially not around young women. But most of us liked Greg irregularly - which is to say we liked him when he wasn't a source of embarrassment - because he was usually interesting, often funny and fearless in his own way. His fearlessness was not so much bravery as indifference to anything he thought was stupid, trivial or short of simple, common sense. His concept of stupidity, triviality and common sense, as anyone with common sense might suspect, didn't always match the generally accepted definitions of those terms.

Greg was tall for the time, probably over six feet, but his body was frail, the result of some unspecific lung condition that combined with superior intelligence and judgment to keep him from enlisting with us. He vaguely resembled the late actor James Stewart - still seen on television every Christmas in a sappy, old movie - and had an unruly head of dark brown hair that was usually combed but never tidy. He always wore long-sleeved shirts, buttoned at the wrists even in the middle of sweltering St. Louis summers, and I assumed he did it to cover his exceedingly pale, thin arms. Jerry thought Greg's ailment, marked by high and persistent fevers before his recovery, was the source of his rampant horniness. My guess was that he simply wanted something he wasn't getting, and he wasn't getting it because his salty language and persistent sarcasms put off most of the young women in a position to give it to him. And the others were either mildly curious or amused, but not usually disposed in a manner that would have produced the result Greg sought. His problem, I think, was that he didn't understand that his vocabulary was a little explicit for the time, and his purpose would have been better served had he found softer words and used them in an agreeable manner.

When the five of us trundled off to Marine boot camp at Parris Island, South Carolina to sweat and strain through several months of military browbeating that changed our attitudes for life, Greg remained at home to amuse himself at major league baseball games and with horse races at tracks across the broad, ponderous, sewage-laden Mississippi River in Illinois. The National

League Cardinals and the American League Browns played at Sportsman's Park, an old baseball stadium built long before the era of lavish corporate suites and never in my recollection used for other sports, concerts or large religious assemblies. The team owners were probably just as greedy as they were in later years, but the ballplayers had not yet had an opportunity to join them in what someone has called the conflict between billionaires and millionaires. And anyone who cared couldn't have imagined, let alone known, that the Browns, despite poor seasons and dwindling attendance, would decline to the point where, in 1953, they would be moved to Baltimore and transformed into something called the Orioles.

There were several racetracks on the Illinois side of the river where the activity was legal, and other entertainment forms - whorehouses, road houses and combinations of both - that weren't supported by statute but got little pressure from the authorities. In Missouri, on the other hand as well as on the other side of the river, there were no races and the city bars, sealed hermetically on Sundays, closed relatively early during the week. There were certainly whorehouses and illegal afterhours bars in St. Louis, but they were operated with a discretion not needed in Illinois.

The Missouri state legislature in Jefferson City - before redistricting imposed a more cosmopolitan attitude - was dominated by rural interests who thought churchgoing was preferable to drinking and whore-mongering. Or, that was their public posture if not always their private practice.

There were both harness and thoroughbred racetracks near East St. Louis in Illinois, although the term thoroughbred may have been a stretch in describing some of the nags that got stuffed into those starting gates. The quality of the animals was of small concern to Greg, who was attracted solely by the gambling. He loved to gamble, but his limited resources and native intelligence told him it was a sucker's game. Knowing that, he devised a system suited to his personal needs and based on the assumption that gamblers get into trouble mainly through greed, desperation or both. He bet the favorites to show, an approach that wasn't particularly clever and wasn't likely to make him wealthy but usually paid his expenses for the day, mainly bus fare, track admission and a hot dog. On a really good day, he sometimes managed to get a cold beer, too. And on the long bus rides home, which required several transfers, he read book after book before he packed himself off to the University at Columbia where Jerry and I were reunited with him when we were discharged from the Marine Corps two years later. The Corps, which usually required three or four year enlistments, provided two year hitches for us at a time, someone told me, when the military power brokers tried to enlarge the ranks in an effort to get a more abundant Congressional appropriation.

Dating to 1839, the University of Missouri is billed as the oldest land grant university west of the Mississippi River, assuming the billers halt that claim at the Pacific Ocean. It was 109 years old when Jerry and I first arrived, not even a mature school in U.S. terms when you consider the Ivy League and a mere puppy compared with some of the foreign institutions. Cambridge and Oxford Universities in England -which are almost as old as the English language itself - as well as the University of Paris in France were founded in the 12th century and other schools still in operation were begun in the 1300s at

Rome and Prague. In the western hemisphere, the National University of Mexico was established in 1551. And that's just the short list. But we modern, immigrated Americans should not be held responsible for the failure of the Indians to grasp the concept of higher education.

At the time and before the system included schools in St. Louis, Kansas City and Zeus-knows-where, the University was mainly centered on two adjoining areas in Columbia, the Red Campus - named for its red, brick buildings and not for any political persuasion - and the White Campus with its white, stone academic halls. The older red campus surrounded six ionic columns on the greensward called Francis Quadrangle, all that remains of the University's first administrative building that was erected in 1840 and destroyed by fire 52 years later. The majestic effect of those surviving columns, I sometimes think, justified loss of the old building.

Columbia itself was originally called Smithton when it became an identifiable community in 1819. The name was changed to its present form a couple of years later when it was designated the county seat, and its original prosperity was based on selling provisions and such to westward-bound immigrants traveling Boone's Lick Trail, which eventually joined the Santa Fe, Oregon and California Trails.

I was drinking beer one freshman night with Greg, Jerry and another student friend, Jim Kelly, at The Stable, a former military barracks transformed into a saloon outside Columbia that had nothing beyond its name, and a permanent aroma that suggested animal urine, to do with horses. Jim, too, had recently left the Marine Corps and was from suburban St. Louis, but we had not known him before our meeting a few months earlier. We were seated in a booth, stacking our empty glasses along a ledge on the wall and conducting a discussion that would have made idle conversation seem profound. A couple of beer pitchers, recently filled, sat in their own puddles on the tabletop, an old, unfinished wood surface with hundreds of carved initials, some with dates, that recorded the history of the saloon. I'd read that soldiers of ancient Greece had carved their initials and other things on the still more ancient pyramids as they passed through Egypt, which tells me there's a strong inclination - even among lowly university undergraduates - to leave a permanent record in an impermanent world. There's also an inclination - particularly among university undergraduates - to create a scruffier environment than the one they found.

It was between semesters and we were the only customers there, sitting contentedly in a blue-gray pall of smoke created by our own Chesterfields, Camels and Lucky Strikes until a rough-looking bunch of bikers arrived, shattering the tranquility, first with their large machines as they rumbled onto the snowless but frozen gravel parking lot and, subsequently, with their raucous entry into the building through the beat-up front door. There were at least a dozen of them and the thunder of their boots on the wood floor sent shivers through the flimsy structure, making the rows of empty glasses on our ledge tinkle ever so slightly. The bikers all wore dirty jeans and some kind of studded black leather, either belts, wristbands or caps. I spotted an assortment of tattoos, visible on hands as they removed their gloves and on thick necks and other exposed body areas, and knew instantly we had what amounted to a motorcycle cliché on our hands. It was a little like a bad movie, but without popcorn. Within a few minutes, they gathered around our booth and within a few additional minutes tried to pick a fight with us. We were elected, I'd guess, because we were the only ones there and because that's what they did for recreation. They were also ugly drunk and heavily outnumbered us, an advantage I'm sure they enjoyed but didn't really need. I hadn't been in a fight since Marine boot camp when a misunderstanding got me into a tussle with another recruit who outweighed me by 90 pounds. The outcome of the fight was inconclusive, but I was sore for three days. I had the impression these motorcycle thugs wouldn't have been satisfied with only three days of soreness. They sought blood and the blood they sought was ours.

A burly, red-headed goon, who smelled like he hadn't showered since puberty, turned out to be their spokesman. With profound ineloquence, he told us we were less than excrement and invited us outside for a good thumping. One of his buddies stood behind him muttering something incomprehensible to me and loudly passing occasional wind. He had a bowel comparable to a test tunnel at the Jet Propulsion Laboratory and he made no effort to control the wild sounds and vile smelts produced by some extraordinary chemistry and a diet, I was certain, of incredible impurity. It could have been a secret weapon had nature not made it a secret impossible to keep. The dope, I thought, was going to gas us to death.

At the same time, one of the other miscreants - a pale, gangly chap with a large, undistinguished nose and a bad complexion - was especially vicious. He was anxious to get us outside where, he said, the blood wouldn't stain the floor. I would have enjoyed getting him alone anywhere, and to hell with the floor. He was, I could tell, one of those shaky people who garner their courage, what little they have, from the mob. Alone, he would have faded into the nearest shadow.

The rest of the pack, meanwhile, were milling around our booth, spewing curses, grunts and other distinctly menacing sounds. We - meaning our small, beleaguered group - muttered our individual replies and stood up inside the booth, knowing we didn't have a prayer against this rabble from nowhere and feeling the wooden benches press against the backs of our legs because there wasn't enough room to stand fully erect. We tried to put on a brave front but we were likely one of the sorrier sights in recent memory. Despite that, I wasn't surprised to see Greg still seated, placidly sipping his beer until the redhead spoke directly to him. "You comin'?" he asked, his voice a surly, rasping personification of pure malevolence. He was also scratching his butt.

"Nope," Greg said. The man looked at him, surprised, I thought, and pursued the matter. He wanted to know if Greg was a yellow dog or some other form of cowardly beast? "Sure, all of those things, and you're some kind of knucklehead," Greg replied.

At this point in their conversation I was certain, just as I was sure Jerry and Jim were certain, that we were going to get beaten half to death and that even worse was in store for Greg. Our prospects, it seemed, had all the ear-marks of a real party-stopper. As it turned out, we weren't beaten at all, a happy circumstance brought about by the arrival of Lou, part owner of the joint and a person of significant proportions, from behind the bar where he'd witnessed the whole, sad mess. He chased the gang away single-handed and, as the old saying so sweetly goes, saved our bacon. The baseball bat in his big hand and the gun-like bulge in his waistband, covered by an apron but abundantly apparent, probably loaned credibility to his six feet, several inches and 250 more or less solid pounds. He had once played football on a University team that was alleged to have gone to the Cotton Bowl after a successful season, a feat not achieved in our recollection by any of the recent teams. Lou, I later thought, saved us a lot of grief, but he was probably motivated by the simple fact we all had large bar tabs and he was only protecting his investment. In my book, it was sufficient justification for the capitalist system.

Greg barely noticed the divine nature of our salvation, but Jerry, Jim and I knew we had dodged the bullet. The relieved expressions on our faces must have said: "That was close." As we settled in for a fresh round of beers, Greg mumbled something about "those knuckleheads." I could still hear the distant throatiness of a dozen motorcycles racing away into the winter night.

DOS

Greg was still alive the night I got stupid drunk in Taxco, mainly out of jealousy driven anger and an essential immaturity I should have outgrown by then. I was approaching 22 and had established a relationship in Mexico with a 36-year-old American woman generally considered attractive. She was a brunette with a summer tan and a trim figure as well as an affluent husband and two young daughters at home in Dallas. I vaguely understood and cared not at all that her interest in me had something to do with an unwillingness to accept the inevitability of aging. She sought surrogate youth and I was the nearest young male when she arrived in Mexico, which proves a couple of things. We all get lucky once in a while, and geography can be your friend.

Her name was Laura Chase and we were at a gathering that night hosted by Janet Joslyn, the matriarchal sponsor of the art workshop group that had brought me and several dozen others to Mexico for the summer. A New York gallery owner with long personal and business ties to Mexico, Janet had gathered a motley assemblage of teachers, students, painters, a lone but apparently not lonely photographer and some, like me, whose classification was not too specific. Most of us had learned of the workshop through ads in several art magazines.

In her early 60s, Janet was modestly plump and gregarious in that restrained way that sometimes marks a person who has dealt for years with those of wealth and prominence. It was, I think, an acquired rather than inherited skill in her case. In Mexico, she liked to affect native costume, wearing those brightly colored skirts and shawls, and an assortment of rings and other trinkets fashioned from the native silver. With her smooth, dark complexion that barely revealed delicate crows-feet, and straight, black hair pulled tightly back into a symmetrical bun, she looked to me like a modern concept of Aztec royalty.

I was having a fine time that evening among congenial people in a popular bar near the zocalo or public square. The general mood was festive, appropriate to the saint's day celebration going on outside where, through broad, open windows, you could see fireworks against the dark sky and hear the crackling explosions that accompanied an overlapping series of white and pink starbursts. The first time I heard those sounds, awakening from a late nap shortly after my arrival in Taxco, I thought the Mexicans had begun another revolution.

Laura and I were at Janet's table with others, including Laura's cousin, Mary Elizabeth Roberts, a woman named Marie Pritchard and two men, Jack Doby and Frank Mirabella. Mary Beth had accompanied Laura on the trip to provide both companionship and an aura of respectability for their family's sake. A high school art teacher, Mary Beth was slender to the edge of skinny with short, curly hair, once blonde, and a drawl that closely matched her cousin's languid speech. They were friends as well as relatives and both were competent painters, as I was to discover, although their work was as different in style as their appearance and personalities. Laura called herself a "sophisticated primitive," which was her idea of a joke but also served to notify anyone who cared that she was schooled and knew what she was doing. Mary Beth didn't call herself anything, but her work, I later learned, was big, bold and colorful, a surprise considering her quiet, almost reclusive manner. It made you wonder what was going on inside that head of hers.

Marie Pritchard and Jack Dobie were New York painters who taught at one of the prominent art schools. They had once been lovers, we were to discover later, and remained friends, just as they remained married to their original spouses, who were not with them on this trip. As far as physical appearance was concerned, they could have been drawn from a common gene pool. Both were about 50, possibly younger, with light brown, graying hair, rather sharp features, and each was a little under middle height for their respective genders. But that was where the resemblance ran out. Marie was permanently on edge, a neurotically engaging woman suffering from, among other things, a kind of painter's block that kept her, at least at the time, from completing any serious work.

Jack, originally from some mountain-bound community in Colorado, was laid back to the point of comatose. Nothing seemed to disturb his essential placidity. He rarely spoke, which is possibly why we didn't notice his absence for three days later that summer when he went off into the mountains alone to explore Indian villages in the area. He apparently enjoyed the experience, but the language barrier proved to be his most difficult obstacle. He could barely communicate his most essential needs and, as a result, ate nothing but soup for the entire period. Sopa was one of the few words in his Spanish vocabulary.

Frank Mirabella was our resident Spanish instructor. He had lived in Mexico since before the second world war, although his speech suggested origins on the U.S. east coast, perhaps New Jersey. He liked to tell anecdotes, particularly when he drank, but he carefully avoided references to his own background. I got the impression he had something to hide, but it also occurred to me that his manner may have simply been a ploy to create mystery where, in reality, there was none. Those alternatives, I suppose, are a little mystery in their own right.

We had been drinking, without food, for some time when we were joined by an acquaintance of Janet's, who sat down and soon began to direct most of his attention to Laura. He was a tall, suave-looking American in his early 40s who had just returned from Italy at a time when non-military European travel by North Americans was unusual, if not exotic. He wore an ascot and a dark blazer, something of a contrast to all the short-sleeved shirts and blouses on everyone else in the bar. I recall, particularly, his voice had that unctuous quality some mistook for urbanity, and his general manner seemed to attract the women in our small circle. Naturally, I knew him instantly for the phony jerk the others failed to recognize.

I said little and drank a lot as the newcomer, whose name never lodged in my memory bank, monopolized the table conversation, paying increasingly personal attention to Laura, who absorbed his line like a thick paper towel in a pool of spilt milk. He lit her cigarettes with his gold lighter and had the especially annoying habit of confiding occasional remarks to her alone. I wanted to set his pants afire with my aluminum Zippo.

As time passed, my patience passed with it and I began to make stupid little comments crudely designed to provoke some kind of confrontation with the man. I tried to contradict almost everything he said and I affected a sarcasm I couldn't have carried off effectively on my soberest day. My obnoxiousness eventually reached the point where it couldn't be ignored. Luckily for me, Janet diffused the situation with the skill of a seasoned mediator. She looked at me, smiling nicely, and ask: "Dear, would you get me a Compari? The service this evening is dreadful." I would, indeed, and did, which saved me from further embarrassment, but not from the further opportunity to get my face punched silly.

I went to the bar to get Janet's drink and found Tony, who owned the place, engaged in an argument with a surly patron. The fiesta outside had ended, but the faint smell of spent fireworks permeated the room, delivered by a soft, steady breeze that flowed in through the generous windows. Laura and I had come to like Tony in the few weeks we'd been in Taxco, mostly because we were usually in the bar every night and he had been an especially courteous host. He invariably sent us nightcaps near the end of the evenings and he treated Laura with a Latin formality that flattered her and didn't nauseate me. His companion, if that's the word, was an English woman called Betty, who had left the hardscrabble life in post-war London, where the rations were still short and the living drab, for a more salubrious climate. She found it and Tony, and I found both of them confronting this oaf at the bar that night.

Barely aware that Tony's antagonist weighed in at more than 200 pounds - which is to say he was burly as well as surly - I approached the two as they glared at each other. "Do you need any help with this clown?" I offered, not giving the slightest consideration to the nature of the help I might be called upon to render. Tony, who hadn't noticed my somewhat wobbly approach, looked at me and his scowl slowly changed to an appreciative smile. "No," he replied, "but thank you. I have many friends here and I can handle this matter."

And handle it he apparently did, but I don't know how. I acquired Janet's Campari, disgusting stuff that it is, and returned to the table to find the tall stranger gone forever from our lives and conversation. He disappeared with the efficiency with which he'd arrived, and it seemed to make no difference to anyone, including Laura. My behavior, which I recognized the next day as less than distinguished, had also gone largely unnoticed, a lucky break I willingly accepted. You don't look a gift horse in the mouth or anywhere else, I've heard.

The confrontation at the bar, though, was an entirely different matter. In the light of day, I began to understand I didn't know much about the man in the argument with Tony. I didn't know if he'd been right or wrong or if he was a good, bad or indifferent person. I didn't know if he was alone or with friends or if he was unarmed or laden with pistols and knives. I knew he was big, but I didn't know if he was tough and, most importantly, I knew nothing of his capacity for violence. Not knowing all those things, it occurred to me I could have been shot, disemboweled, beaten to a bloody pulp or worse. And aside from all that, there was a final irony in the whole sordid affair.

Tony, who knew nothing of my jealousy-induced stupidity and was too preoccupied to notice my drunkenness that balmy evening, was genuinely moved by my offer of assistance. He saw what I did as a courageous act of friendship rather than the blatant commission of foolishness that it really was. As a result, I couldn't pay for a drink in that bar for the rest of the summer, and Tony expressed further gratitude by putting his arm around my shoulders and calling me "amigo" at the slightest provocation. And while I didn't care for all this overt chumminess, I accepted it as the price to be paid for my craven deception.

THREE

I was obliviously settled for the summer in Taxco when the Peoples Democratic Republic of North Korea attack the Republic of South Korea at dawn on June 25, 1950 with sufficient ferocity to overwhelm the southern capital, Seoul, three days later. By the end of August, the northerners occupied all of South Korea except the area around Pusan, an important port city. The United Nations Security Council, despite a boycott by its Russian member, mustered troops from 15 nations under the unified command of General Douglas MacArthur to repel the invasion. As these historic events developed, my life ran a leisurely course devoid of newspapers and other topical information sources. I was vaguely aware of the hostilities, just as those around me in Taxco must have been, but I don't remember a single comment or discussion about the deadly activities on the Korean peninsula. We stuck our collective heads in the Mexican sand, and trusted that no one would kick our butts.

General MacArthur eventually made a daring landing with U.S. and South Korean marines some 200 miles behind enemy lines at the same time he launched an offensive from Pusan that pushed the invaders all the way to the Yalu River, the frontier between Korea and Chinese

Manchuria. The General's initial tactical brilliance was soon overshadowed by a colossal strategic miscalculation regarding Chinese intentions. Those red-yellow devils swarmed down on the United Nations forces and sent them reeling back to where they'd been. The good guys, us, eventually recovered and the war soon settled into one of those largely static affairs where people, military and civilian, still get killed but not much real estate changes hands. It was a trick mastered early in the century during the first world war by a coterie of arrogant French, British and German generals whose pompous stupidity and flagrant disregard for human life enabled them to heavily deplete an entire generation of young men, not to mention a few older ones, with massed frontal attacks against largely impregnable defenses. They also deflowered a great deal of landscape, which - unlike the young soldiers - was with time restored.

MacArthur, whose virtues and faults were always on a grand scale, seemed to value the lives of his troops and often made decisions over his long military career that held battle casualties to a minimum. His decision to test the Chinese in Korea was not, however, one of them.

Eventually, the Korean War would destroy perhaps three and a half to four millions, including civilians, on both sides. There were 142,000 Americans and 17,000 from other UN forces who died in this war to defend a right-wing dictatorship from a left-wing dictatorship. But South Korea was our dictatorship and the North Koreans were allied with the Russians. The Chinese got involved despite their antipathy to the Russians and more for geographical than geopolitical reasons.

MacArthur and his troops apparently got too close to suit a bunch of communist hardheads not too far removed from a long, bloody war with the Japanese as well as an equally bloody civil war that sent their Chinese nationalist enemies packing to Taiwan.

The whole tiresome Korean matter would not play out during my summer in Mexico. The fighting ended in July, 1953, but the peace negotiations dragged on until 1972 when the two Korean governments agreed to seek unification of the peninsula by peaceful means. By that time, MacArthur was long dead, the United States had found other trouble in Vietnam and my recollections of that Mexican summer were beginning to merge with dimming memories of my childhood and other times gone by.

Those memories were of times and events that for better or worse shaped my character (or the lack of it) and personality as surely as my genetic background also contributed to those qualities, giving me certain capacities and depriving me of others. I'm only calling attention to the obvious when I tell you everyone's early years have a profound influence on their subsequent lives. In my case, I was born into reasonably prosperous circumstances only a year before the 1929 stock market crash and ensuing economic depression ruined any chance I had of becoming a spoiled rich kid. Instead, I became a spoiled kid from the lower middle class.

I spent my first four years in the miniscule southern town where my father had lived his entire life and where he had brought my mother after their marriage in 1925. Mum, who had grown up in a northern city, was not expecting the reality of a small, southern community in the 1920s, a town where all the lights were out by nine at night and where, if you didn't chop cotton, there wasn't that much more to do at high noon. She also didn't know that my father - despite his youth and enough southern charm to get her to accept his marriage proposal - had what his family called "a problem." Dad was the center of his family, eldest and most favored among three children, two boys and a girl, but he was also a drunk, a hard fact they (his family) had kept from my mother under the delusion that marriage and responsibility would solve the problem. It didn't, and my father's binges, particularly after my birth, frightened my mother, although the things he did when he was drunk were always self-destructive rather than physically abusive to her. He got into fist fights, almost losing an eye in one brawl, and he destroyed a succession of automobiles without regard to make or model. She finally left him, moving us to St. Louis where she had close relatives and where she had briefly lived and worked as a secretary before their marriage. They subsequently divorced and dad, when I was 10 and he was in his early 30s, blew his brains out with a .38 caliber handgun after a series of failed attempts to achieve sobriety and other virtues. His adult life was short, beginning with a blizzard of drunken nights with drunken friends and ending in one of my grandmother's bedrooms where she sat on the floor with his head cradled in her lap as her son's life slipped away. It reminds me of something I heard a musician say in a radio interview when he was asked what life was like on a long tour where he had to perform night after night in city after city. "It's like life itself," he explained, "fun in the beginning and hell at the end."

I loved my father as any child given half a chance would, and that love was not entirely the result of the vast amounts of ice cream and Coca Cola he bought me during my summer vacations with him in the south. At home, those treats were reserved for special occasions. The power over children of liberally applied sugar probably explains my attempt, when i was about seven or eight, to get my dad to join me for an ice cream cone. I thought once he'd tasted one, he'd never want liquor again.

When he died, my mother, late one raw November night, got a long distance telephone call, which meant trouble in those days before long distance calls became as common as muggings and fast food restaurants. I overheard the conversation from my bedroom down the hall, understood that my father had died but also gathered that we would fly the next day from our St. Louis home to his funeral in Memphis. The prospect of that commercial airline flight in late 1938 erased all concept of death from my thoughts. Earlier in the year, Howard Hughes had flown around the world in record time and Douglas Corrigan, defying the authorities who wouldn't clear him to fly his little plane across the Atlantic, did it anyway and arrived safely in Dublin from the U.S. I needed to fly and if it took a death in the family to make that possible, so be it. I made my pact with the devil, who made certain my mother and I were aboard a Chicago and Southern Airlines DC-3 the next day from the old Lambert Field terminal in St. Louis to Memphis, where my dad's remains remain to this day.

If my summer in Mexico 12 years later was a blissful reverie, my return to the States was a rude awakening. I learned of Greg's death and I learned that two of the four high school friends who had enlisted in the Marines with me, Ned Inglish and Ed Kelly (no relation to Jim), had been called up for Korean military service. They, like General MacArthur, had made a major strategic booboo. They remained in the Marine Corps reserves when we were discharged, probably under the optimistic assumption we'd had two world wars that far in the century and weren't likely to have another one any time soon. That assumption made them subject to recall, which was almost inevitable when the Korean thing broke out during a period when U.S. military forces had been heavily demobilized after the second big war. It was also before the cold war with the Russians had heated up enough to give the military-industrial complex an opportunity to spend and make some really big money. My friends got called up with other reservists, many of them barely trained for what lay ahead.

The other school friend who enlisted with me, Bob Tully, managed to avoid Korea, as Jerry and I did, by avoiding the reserves. I've always assumed that Ned and Ed joined that organization for the monthly allowance it provided, but that's only a guess. Tully went on to graduate from a small university in Illinois and eventually settled in Dallas, where he lived for years without acquiring a drawl or any other detectable evidence of southern residence.

Ned and Ed survived Korea and returned home to live productive lives. In other words, they worked, paid taxes and didn't get sent to prison. Ned barely forgave me for sending cheerful postcards to him from London early the following year while he dodged wintry shellfire in the Orient. My other friend, Ed, didn't have to forgive me for anything because I didn't have his military address.

A British author - Lawrence Durrell, I think, but don't hold me rigidly to it - sought seclusion or serenity or something along those lines after the second world war on one of the Greek islands, where he spent his time writing and generally paying little attention to the outside world. When he finally returned to soggy, old England and began once again to read newspapers, he found, he said, there had been little significant change in the order of things. There had been large events, but it was only more of the same.

That may have been true for Durrell or whoever it was who said it, but it wasn't true for me. The world - both my personal one and that vast accumulation of stuff that spans all those time zones - had been altered in the few months I'd been in Mexico. It was as though I'd driven into and out of a time warp in the little green 1949 Chevrolet that carried me to Taxco and back.

QUATRO

Most of those in Janet's workshop, particularly the younger ones, were housed at the Hotel de la Borda, a rambling structure on the main highway at the edge of town. For some reason I never knew, a few of us were lodged at the Casa Humboldt, built with the intention of permanence in the 1700s and named for the celebrated German naturalist, traveler and statesman, Baron Friedrich Hemrich Alexander von Humboldt, whose overnight stay there in 1803 was sufficient justification to endow the building with his name.

The Baron, who founded something called Comparative Climatology and in later life became a patron of younger scientists and a popularizer of science, made a scientific journey to South America, Cuba and Mexico that took five years (1799-1804) and which covered more than 6,000 miles. Those were rugged miles in those days and he made the trip on foot, horseback and canoe for lack of easier options. He made other scientific expeditions - one to Russian Asia in 1829 - as well as several diplomatic missions for the Prussian government. He died at 90, not a mean feat for someone whose life spanned the latter half of the 18th and first half of the 19th centuries and who insisted on travel in relatively primitive places. He's not to be confused with his older brother, Wilhelm, who was also a distinguished Prussian diplomat and a pioneer in Ethnolinguistics, which could surely rival Comparative Climatology as an arcane field of investigation. There must have been some kind of genetic predisposition in the family for that kind of thing, but Friedrich's achievements and durability, in any event, makes me think they don't make barons like him anymore.

As I recall, the Casa Humboldt is a fortress-like stone building within easy walking distance from the town square. I read later that it had once been a convent and a hospital and after my time there had become the community's first movie theater and, eventually, a museum. In 1950, its stout, wooden front door, almost flush with the cobblestone street, could only be unlocked with an iron key about six inches long and, I'd guess, about a quarter pound in weight. Put that in your trouser pocket, sir, and you'll either be the envy or the embarrassment of your companions.

My room, probably typical, was spacious, whitewashed and sparsely furnished, with a gracefully arched opening that led onto a narrow balcony framed with brilliant red bougainvillea. Beyond, a profusion of tile roofs - mandated by law to retain the town's Spanish colonial integrity - were visible up the hillsides. There was a primitive bathroom between my quarters and Marie Pritchard's room, and we were supplied with hot water for half an hour every afternoon. The supply went largely untapped because I didn't want to regulate my schedule to the water supply and also because I soon learned that cold showers could cleanse my body without any detectable effect on my libido.

Once, while contemplating the Humboldt's history, I wondered if some physical vestige of the illustrious baron - perhaps a minute fragment of pubic hair dislodged when he undressed that single night in Taxco - survived in some remote, hermetic crevice in the old building. And if it could be found and identified, what useful information could we retrieve from its DNA, color or texture? None, probably, but it was only a random thought.

Laura, Mary Beth, Marie and Jack also stayed at the Humboldt, which was managed by a young German baroness we called Trixie. She was a tall woman with braided blonde hair, almost beautiful in her imposing Teutonic way and in no manner related, even by marriage, to the historic baron. Trixie had an infant daughter destined, I was sure, to resemble her mother, and a husband, another baron, who ran a museum of some kind in Mexico City and whose absence from the Humboldt seemed more or less permanent. Meanwhile, she ran the household with effortless efficiency, or so it seemed to someone unaware of the effort needed to supervise a reasonably large establishment with a continuous round of paying guests who'd been promised several meals a day and a pleasant environment. Those meals, I thought, were particularly good, an unlikely combination of regional Mexican cooking and Trixie's strong German influence. My palate was unsophisticated and not too far removed from military messhalls, but the others, older and more experienced in culinary matters, also liked the food. And you could eat anything served at the Humboldt without fear of the dreaded flux that afflicted so many visitors to Mexico.

The building was old, inefficient and difficult to manage but, thanks to Trixie, was a charming wonder from its immaculate kitchen to the fresh flowers that graced its public areas. When I learned many years later the place had been turned into a movie theater, however briefly, it only confirmed my developing conviction that the world was becoming less civilized. Movies have a place, but I don't think that place is the Casa Humboldt.

Those in the workshop, both students and professionals, ranged in age from their 20s to late 40s with the exception of two retired school teachers, Miss Jamison and Miss Cooper, who were in their early 80s when actuarial tables showed that most people cashed in their eternal chips in their 60s. They had arrived in Mexico aboard what one of them called a "tramp steamer" from the United States. The ladies had come out of that long period in American life when women school teachers were unmarried by board of education and public decree, and when many of them traveled widely on summer vacations. When Stanley found Livingston in the mainly unexplored depths of 19th century Africa, he could just as well have stumbled across a band of wandering American school teachers had the two men not come together in November when classes were in session. The travel, one supposes, was meant to broaden the teachers in an educational way, but I'd bet more than a dollar that the younger teachers used those trips to escape the prying scrutiny of school administrators, family and other high-minded citizens.

The Misses Jamison and Cooper had been almost everywhere in the civilized world and then some, and were still eager to scout those places they had not seen. Their instincts were those of the great explorers but their appearance was more reminiscent of Whistler's mother. I didn't think about it at the time, but they were among the last of a dying breed.

The years have erased my recollection of most of those in the workshop, mainly because I had little contact with them during that summer. I vaguely remember a group of younger ones, about evenly divided between the sexes, that stuck together, and I recall a middle-aged man named Herb, who confessed to Mary Beth one night at a party that he loved her and his wife with equal intensity.

Mary Beth understood his motive - plainly apparent since they'd known each other less than an hour - and the nature of that intensity, perhaps better than old Herb who was a bit sauced, and told him to stick it in the sand. There wasn't much sand short of Acapulco, but he got the message and, subsequently, left her alone. We - meaning the Humboldt guests - got the story from Mary Beth the next morning at breakfast. There were few secrets at the dining table, although the nature of the intelligence almost always dealt with someone who had done something or something that had happened the prior day. It was mainly overnight, local news that came to you with your eggs racheros.

The Humboldt would have been a rumor mill had it not been for the accuracy of the gossip that dominated mealtime conversation. The workshop and the expatriate community around it were small worlds, but they were worlds teeming with varieties of small-time intrigue. The temporary sexual liaisons among the workshop members alone would have been enough to keep the Humboldt table conversation going for a year. I think it was Marie Pritchard, expert gossip that she was, who learned and subsequently told us that Frank Mirabella, who lived in town apart from the workshop people, had come perilously close to a fatal mistake. He made a move on the English woman, Betty, in full view of Tony, my bar-owning amigo. Frank had adopted and assimilated some of the local cultural characteristics during his long residence in Mexico, but the fiery Latin temperament was beyond him. There was no fire in his belly to compare with Tony's, which is another way to say Frank was surprised when Tony grabbed him by the throat with one hand and pushed the nose of a small revolver into his stomach with the other. The caliber of the gun was a mystery, but it sufficiently impressed Frank to the point where the blood literally drained from his face and he tremblingly assured Tony he'd stay clear of the lovely Betty. I like to think he also wet his pants but there's no real evidence to support that conclusion. Oddly, only Marie and a few others knew about the confrontation, mainly because it happened late at night when the bar was virtually empty, and Tony moved with such swiftness the entire episode only lasted a few minutes. Betty, according to Marie, barely noticed Frank's interest in her, and may have entirely missed Tony's violent but surgically precise reaction. She was filing her fingernails when it all happened, and she still had several nails to finish when Frank, shaken to his toes, left the bar in a hurry. Betty had been through the German aerial attacks on London during the war, and something as pedestrian as a near shooting in some Mexican mountain town wasn't likely to arrest her attention. When you've seen one of the world's great cities ablaze, the prospect of a small whole in an obscure Spanish instructor could well seem trivial.

Frank, I noticed on several occasions over the ensuing weeks, always seemed to be dogging some young woman. I never got to know him that well, nor did I want to, but I had the impression he was one of those men who'd screw anything - without regard to size or shape -

as long as it was female and under 25. At the same time, I later learned from Marie, he had been supported from time to time by older women, usually American widows or divorcees who were seeking something they were unlikely to find in Frank. Frankly, there wasn't much in Frank to find, as far as I was concerned, and it amazed me that he could dupe a woman, any woman, long enough to get money or sex from them. He liked to talk, but he wasn't usually very interesting, and he was short, ordinary and had the annoying habit of chewing on his lower lip. His fluency in Spanish, I thought, was his only virtue, and my ignorance of the language made it impossible to confirm even that. I was particularly put off by his proselytizing political conservatism, which he glibly revealed was a reaction to an equally ardent advocacy of socialism or something like it when he was young. He was one of those people who go from one extreme to the other without regard for the center, always sure they know how to remedy the world's problems. I was neither conservative, liberal or otherwise, much as I am today, and didn't care what anyone else was as long as they didn't try to force their views down my throat. Or up my ass. But I didn't (and don't) care for people who are so cocksure they know what's good for me they're willing to kill me to prove it. Frank was that kind of person.

I also learned late in the summer that he'd made a feeble pass at Laura, an event that was kept from me by Laura, Mary Beth and Marie under the very correct assumption that I would have assaulted him. By the time I heard about it, too much time had elapsed for any kind of effective confrontation, and I wasn't anxious to embarrass myself again with some precipitant act. There's some fundamental law that says only a fool will make a fool of himself twice in the same summer. I simply avoided Frank those final weeks, secure in the knowledge he was a known ass-hole. He was also a bore and I was certain, without knowing much of the language, that he was just as boring in Spanish.

FIVE

The rain had been heavy and unrelenting on that mid-August day in 1946, and it continued into the evening we left St. Louis for Marine Corps boot camp in South Carolina. My enlistee friends and I took separate public buses to Union Station, where our recruiters had told us we'd have Pullman accommodations, considered posh at the time, for the two-day train trip south. Instead, we joined a larger group of recruits, perhaps 30 in all, aboard an ancient troop sleeper with three-high bunks and a history that probably went back to the first world war. Or beyond.

We were told the torrential rains had inflicted considerable damage throughout the region, washing out road-beds and bridges, and delaying in-bound trains that may have included those Pullmans the Corps had promised us. Even the sad substitute we boarded, which began taking on heavy, black soot through the open windows as soon as we were underway, was routed north into Illinois for more than 100 miles before someone could identify clear track for the now extended trip south. The journey turned into more than three hot, grimy days aboard a vessel that rolled, pitched and creaked more than you'd expect from the Pinta, Nina or Santa Maria.

By the time we got to Beaufort, South Carolina, near the recruit training base at Parris Island, we were a bunch of sweat-soaked, soot-laden, worn-out teenagers who didn't know it would only get worse before the day was over.

We piled off that train, momentarily relieved before we learned what was in store for us, and were lined up into our first military formation by four veteran Marines whose purpose was to meet and intimidate us before we got the impression we'd stumbled into a democratic organization. We stayed in that formation, standing at rigid attention under a blazing afternoon sun, until several in our ranks passed out. They simply crumpled to the ground and were left there while our Marine greeters barked orders and information that mainly told us we were about to be "snapped out of our civilian shit."

These shit snappers were impressive, seemingly impervious to the heat in starched, sharply creased khakis and an authoritarian bearing that enabled them to take immediate control of what a short time earlier had been an unruly mob of ex-high schoolers. We didn't know it at the time, but they were veterans of the recent Pacific war against the Japanese.

Eventually, we were loaded, much like cattle but without as much courtesy, on trucks for the ride to the island where we were put through a process and a place called "Sanitation," a spare facility presided over by a tense buck sergeant with all the charm of an executioner during the French Reign of Terror. We were made to surrender our filthy clothes, shower and have our heads shorn to bare skin, which accounts for the term "skin head" used then to describe a raw recruit. That rawness was underscored by the stiff, green dungarees and dungaree jackets we were issued along with color-matched underwear and heavy boots we soon learned to call "boondockers." In the months ahead, the dungarees would slowly fade to a salty color, partially from heavy wear and partially from constant scrubbing with stiff-bristled brushes to erase the recruit image. The boondockers, too, would turn from tawny to dark brown from hard wear on the drill fields and sand pits and from forced marches as well as from the oil we painstakingly rubbed into them to eradicate any trace of newness. We understood intuitively that all that training, discipline and other effort would be wasted if we didn't look the part.

Our platoon, made up of about 70 very young men from cities and towns, villages and farms east of the Mississippi River and north of the Mason-Dixon line, was still a pretty sorry-looking bunch when Master Gunnery Sergeant Pilsner gave us our first formal inspection. As we stood at attention, our M-1 rifles at shoulder arms, he looked at us sternly and explained his world view. "I hate civilians," he said with a deep, rumbling voice. "My mother was a civilian." He paused for dramatic effect, and then delivered the punch line. "I hate my mother." The sergeant may have hated his mother for any number of reasons or he may have lied to us. But the performance was mainly convincing and no one in the platoon openly questioned his sincerity. All I heard was a muffled "Jesus" from somewhere in the ranks.

Gunny Sergeant Pilsner administered our first inspection, but corporals Bray and Anderson were our drill instructors, which meant they had more immediate power over us than God or Harry Truman. Bray was a lean, taciturn Pennsylvanian and Anderson was lean and taciturn from somewhere else. I suspected they'd been to Lean and Taciturn School, an institution, I further suspected, that was run by the Corps for the exclusive training of future drill instructors. There was a sign on the front gate of the school, I'd bet, that warned fat, talkative people to keep out.

Bray and Anderson had fought the Japanese in the South Pacific and both would leave the Corps soon after they had trained our platoon. Before they were snapped back into their civilian shit, however, they made certain we were snapped out of ours. They did much of it to the rhythmic chant of Marine Corps cadence, which was devised to keep troops in step during close order drill, marches and other foolishness. "Won, hup, areap," it began, and continued in a monotonous succession of won, hup, areaps that we would hear, before long, in our sleep. When I first heard it I thought Bray was yelling some obscure foreign curse until he told us in plainer English how stupid we were and what was in store for us if we didn't "shape up, god dammit." We shaped up, as I'm sure he knew we would, but it took time.

In all, it took about three months for those two men to bully and browbeat the platoon into shape, which means we were thoroughly trained, conditioned and humiliated into a group that was truly devoid of civilian shit. We learned to dismantle, clean and fire a variety of weapons and toss hand grenades. They made us put on gas masks and take them off in a room filled with tear gas, just to prove, I suppose, that fresh air on the whole is preferable. They made us scramble through sand, muck and water and to "hit the deck" every time Bray or Anderson yelled "air raid." The main problem with all that deck-hitting is that it was usually done in some desolate part of the island where the ample sand, muck and slimy water gunked our rifles, which we had to clean later. And they marched us all day, every day, first in the unrelenting heat of late August and September and into the cooler weather of October and November. We often did close order drill in deep sand, sometimes with one end of our cartridge belts attached to the ends of our rifles. The other end of the belts swung free, especially when the platoon, under orders from Bray or Anderson, wheeled in another direction. The iron clips on those belts thudded against pith helmets and skinned heads every time we were ordered to the right or left flank and especially when one of the corporals commanded a march to the rear. We learned to hate those pith helmets, which were perfect targets for the swinging cartridge belts, and we crushed them flatter than a cheap pizza at the end of boot camp by trampling them under our boondockered feet.

The corporals, early in our training, would sometimes roust us out of our bunks in the middle of the night to sand scrub the barracks floors, either with bricks or toothbrushes. We also learned to clean latrines, mop up almost anything and slosh mashed potatoes onto someone's food tray from two feet away in the course of an obligation called "mess duty." And it certainly was.

These skills were not all that extraordinary when you consider the millions of military men and women who'd done exactly the same thing during the recent war. Once we'd done it, though, it changed our status within the Corps. We were no longer skinheads, figuratively and literally, because our hair had grown into crew cuts, and Bray and Anderson began to treat us with something like mild amusement rather than abject disgust. It occurred to me some years later that these men - Bray, Anderson, Pilsner and their like - were not only competent marines but accomplished actors. They could feign any emotion, adopt any posture or guise they needed to get absolute obedience and attention, sometimes from big, mean, pissed-off recruits. True, they were supported by an organization that would throw your teenage ass into a real jail they called a "brig" if you crossed them, but it was no easy task for a couple of corporals, not much older than their charges, to handle 70 young men, some of them problem cases who'd been shipped off to the Marine Corps by parents or others who wanted to make them someone else's problem.

Not that all the drill instructors and other non-commissioned officers were as young as Bray and Anderson. Or as lean and taciturn. These were the grizzled marines who had served in China and other foreign posts before the second war and were in it from the Japanese attack on Pearl Harbor to the mushroom-clouded end at Hiroshima and Nagasaki. They had entered service during the economic depression of the 1930s when military budgets were spare to non-existent and when it could take years to rise from the rank of private to private first class or from private first class to corporal. And many of those who managed to gain rare promotions, lost them overnight as the result of drunken brawls in far-eastern whorehouses or for other innocuous indiscretions The men who not only survived the war but service before the war were almost mythic figures to the raw recruits of my generation. By the time we arrived on Parris Island, they were beginning to fade into retirement or other forms of dispersal, although many of them were not old by contemporary standards. But they had participated in a turbulent period of history and had seen it from a perspective unknown to the high-ranking politicians, diplomats and military commanders of the time. What U.S president, ambassador or general had stood guard duty at a lonely post in China during the 1930s, staring across a frontier at a Japanese sentry he was destined to fight a few years later in some remote jungle.

I was not cut out for permanent military service, mainly because I don't want to be told how to dress. That and a mild aversion to being shot at. But I respect those who have done it, either out of duty, financial necessity or pure accident, that great instigator of military achievement

My own Marine Corps service was remarkable in only one respect. I enlisted of my own free will and managed to serve during a short period of relative peace between two large, deadly wars. That service and an amateur's interest in history has given me some appreciation for those who saw harder service.

Semper Fi.

SEIS

I had driven to Mexico from my home in St. Louis, where I met two women from Boston by pre-arrangement with those who ran the workshop. The women were paying passengers and another pair of teachers, although they were half the ages of the intrepid Misses Jamison and Cooper, bless their splendid old souls. The Bostonians had traveled to St. Louis by train and spent a night at the old Coronado Hotel, where I met them the following morning and we immediately left for Mexico. We spent five consecutive days together in a relatively small automobile as we traveled southwest, initially through Missouri, Oklahoma and a seemingly unending Texas on two-lane roads that pre-dated the inter-state highway system. At the end of the second day, we spent the night at a motel in Laredo, one of the principal ports of entry into Mexico. The city, across the Rio Grande River from Nuevo Laredo, was founded in 1755 by an officer in the royal Spanish army and its residents have lived under seven different flags. At one time (1839-41), Laredo was the capital of a separate nation someone elected to call The Republic of the Rio Grande. That someone must have been a gringo because the river is known to the Mexicans as the Rio Bravo. The short-lived republic included south Texas and the region that now covers the three northernmost Mexican states.

The river that gave the republic its name and separated us from Mexico on that exceedingly hot second night was 1885 miles long, rising in the San Juan Mountains of southwest Colorado and flowing south through the middle of New Mexico, then generally southeast as the border between Texas and old Mexico. It then makes a big bend and eventually empties into the Gulf of Mexico at Brownsville, Texas and its sister Mexican city, Matamoros. If you don't believe me, you can consult a map.

As soon as we had checked into the motel late that afternoon, I left the women to their own devices and went downtown to the automobile club office to get car insurance for the trip into Mexico. I'd read or been told the Mexican police happily threw Americans into jail and forgot them if they have accidents without coverage. And Mexican jails, I'd heard, were only a little better than Turkish prisons.

The heat that early summer day was intense even by south Texas standards when I eventually finished my business and found refuge at a restaurant counter in an air-conditioned downtown hotel. At that time, Texas had what I assume were local option liquor laws that left some areas bone dry and allowed others to dispense beer, if not the hard stuff. They did, in fact, sell very cold beer at the counter I fortuitously discovered, and I had a number of them as I sat there and wrote postcards, which I'd purchased in the lobby, to everyone I knew and, not unlikely, a few complete strangers. Those frigid beers on that blistering afternoon struck a responsive cord in me after two long days on the road.

I was feeling pretty mellow as I mailed my postcards in the same lobby where I'd bought them and waltzed out of the air-conditioned hotel into the most horrendous heat I'd yet experienced. It was a three-figure warm front that hit me like a bone dry tidal wave, evaporating every drop of spare moisture on my body and proving, once again, that alcohol and excessive outside temperatures, high or low, don't usually mix. My car, like most others of that vintage, wasn't equipped with an air-conditioner, but I made it back to my motel room, which was, and promptly passed out.

I awoke the next morning, surprisingly refreshed, and an hour or so later we crossed the bridge into Nuevo Laredo and then pressed on through the desert of northern Mexico as well as through tropical zones and into the mountains before we finally reached Mexico City several days later. I remember my companions as pleasant enough, but I have no recollection these many years later of their faces, names or of our conversations during that long, mainly hot trip. I recall, in fact, only three trivial events on the journey.

The first occurred on an interminable strip of desert highway somewhere between Nuevo Laredo and Monterrey, a large industrial city in the northeastern part of the country. The afternoon heat was substantial and the vista was uncompromisingly monotonous, nothing but wasteland, cacti and an occasional village with a sign urging us in Spanish to drink Coca Cola. As we barreled down the road on one particularly barren stretch, we passed a lone burro - one of those small donkey-like pack animals - standing at roadside with a penile erection that was preposterous both for its enormous size and for the remoteness of any possibility it would soon serve the purpose nature intended. I doubt a burro's erect penis - even one that almost touched the ground under its own ponderous weight, as this one did - would elicit much embarrassment today, but in 1950 it was not a subject much discussed by casual acquaintances of different genders. We all saw the huge instrument, but no one said a word about it as the horny beast diminished to a dot and then disappeared in my rear view mirror.

The second event I recall from the trip happened at the hotel where we elected to stay on our first night in Mexico. I was in a short line at the registration desk, standing behind a North American who was using the most halting Spanish ever perpetrated on that euphonious language in a vain effort to communicate something to a tall man with a neatly groomed black mustache behind the counter. The gringo, it seemed, was having his first encounter with another culture. Showing considerable patience, the desk clerk heard him out and then said: 'Sir, I think it would be to our mutual advantage if you spoke English." And, indeed, it was.

My third and final recollection from that trip evokes our arrival in Mexico City, fortunately for us late on a Sunday afternoon when the city traffic - terrific even then, although without the deadly smog that would one day afflict the area - was relatively light. We were tired of the car, tired of the road and, probably, tired of each other. As I struggled with a city map in an increasingly frustrating effort to find the small hotel where the workshop members were to assemble, I drove until we were hopelessly lost in a vast metropolitan maze. At that point, I began to seek directions from anyone on the streets willing to give them. Unfortunately, no one I approached spoke English, and my Spanish preparation for our arrival in the city was limited to a single request for directional information. "Done este Marcella veinte-ocho?" which was the hotel address. The question was good enough, but I failed to anticipate that I would be unable to understand the answer unless it was rendered in English.

I eventually covered a large area of a very big city and conducted unproductive conversations with a half dozen people before I finally found a young man who understood the question and knew the answer. He was familiar with the hotel and its location and would gladly show us the way... for a price. I agreed and he joined us in the car where he directed me to the first corner for a right turn down to the next corner for another right turn to the hotel. Marcella veinte-ocho, it turned out, was on the opposite side of the same block where I had agreed to pay the man for directions. Big city, big coincidence, I must have thought as I shelled out the pesos.

A small, well-kept, cosmopolitan establishment, the hotel was our base for a week-long schedule of activities that began the first evening with a cocktail reception where everyone got acquainted and at least half plastered. I met Laura, Mary Beth and, perhaps, Marie and Jack, although the precise events of the evening are somewhat clouded by time, tequila and the accumulated effects of five long days on the road. I had also driven that day from lower elevations to Mexico City, which is more than 7,000 feet above sea level and usually requires a period of acclimatization to the altitude. Drinking one's self into a misty haze is not, of course, a good way to acclimate to altitude, as I discovered the next morning when I awoke and tried to get out of bed on rubbery legs. I settled back for a few more hours of sleep, which repaired most of the damage and enabled me to attend an archaeological lecture at the national university. Outside the lecture hall, I saw an unoccupied scaffold that shortly before had supported the painter, Diego Rivera, as he produced yet another of the large, ubiquitous murals that cover so many public walls in his country.

Rivera, who still had seven years to live, had not only put his politically pointed paintings on some of Mexico's most important edifices, including the National Palace, but had done major works in the United States for Rockefeller Center in New York and the Detroit Institute of Arts. The Rockefeller Center mural, "Man at the Crossroads," was intentionally destroyed by its commissioners and later recreated at the Palace of Fine Arts in Mexico City, mainly because one of the figures Rivera painted had a striking and certainly intentional resemblance to Lenin. In Detroit, where he filled a large room - now called the Rivera Court - with paintings that show industrial America in what can reasonably be called a harsh light, he got support from Edsel Ford, son of old Henry, founder of Ford Motor Company. Art surely rivals politics in its ability to attract strange bedfellows.

We went on in the ensuing week to the usual tourist attractions, including Teotihuacan where I dutifully climbed to the lofty summit of the Pyramid of the Sun, an arduous task even when you're young and in reasonably good condition. I recalled the steepness of that ancient monument more than 30 years later when I made another difficult ascent, that time up a Mayan pyramid at Chichen Itza in the Yucatan. The two structures were built by different peoples many centuries apart and in different areas of what is now Mexico. But I think some cosmic force, transcending time and cultures, compelled both societies to construct these huge things for a single purpose. The objective was to make it as painful as possible for all the future tourists dumb enough to climb these vast rock piles.

We also saw the castle in Chapultepec Park, atop a hill stormed by U.S. marines during the Mexican-American war in 1847. As a former marine, I was familiar with that episode in our national history because the Corps had taught me the red stripe on the dress blue uniform trousers symbolized that bloody assault. I assumed the red stripe symbolized American blood, leaving the young Mexican cadets who defended the place to find their own symbol. It was, no doubt, the least of their problems.

That week, we toured historical buildings and churches by the blockload as well as museums, theaters and markets. We went to Xochimilco, the so-called "Floating Gardens" which I informally christened The Floating Garbage Dump for the amount of unidentifiable debris floating amidst the flower-laden boats. Some of us went to a burlesque show where a large-breasted woman, wearing a blue gown that covered her ample body from neck to ankles, paraded back and forth across the stage in profile while a sexually-deprived male audience cheered, whistled and stomped more enthusiastically than you would have expected had they been watching a band of naked virgins frolicking in clover.

I managed during the week to buy a single gift for a young woman back home I had dated with some regularity. Although we were always friends more than anything else, my gift, revealing as it did something of my character, probably ensured that our relationship would never go any further. I acquired and presented to her on my return a genuine Swiss-made, Mexican coo coo clock, inexpertly carved from cheap wood and stained a hideous dark brown. The young woman accepted the gift and I have occasionally wondered what she did with It. I have also wondered if my taste, over the years, has improved.

We toured every day and some of us partied most of the nights that week in the Valley of Mexico. It was an experience that taught me a couple of lessons I've applied most of my subsequent life. First, never go on a guided tour to anywhere and, second, never refuse a good time if the opportunity is legal and offered without strings. The good times that week began when I met Laura and the others who would compose the Humboldt group. They were people who knew intuitively that industriousness should be applied to both recreation as well as work.

SEVEN

Greg's political views were beyond liberal, but short of direct membership in the Communist Party as another red scare swept across America several years after the United States and the Soviet Union ended their war-time alliance. He did volunteer work for Henry Wallace, who ran as a third party candidate for president in 1948, and he was active with the NAACP and other organizations that had, at the time, more initials than members. He did real work for these groups and he paid them more lip service than some of his friends, including me, could always endure. But those who liked him understood most of the time that he saw injustice and it simply pissed him off. He loved Jackie Robinson, who broke the major league baseball color barrier in 1947 when he joined the old Brooklyn Dodgers. He loved Robinson on two levels, one as a symbol of black progress and the other as an athlete who played his game with great ability under difficult circumstances. "Go, Jackie," was his inevitable comment when the sports sections in the Post-Dispatch or Globe Democrat revealed that Robinson had done something newsworthy. He was also partial to black women, particularly if they could sing. He always referred to Sarah Vaughn as 'Sarah, baby," and his appreciation for her virtuosity was heavily tinged with vicarious lust.

Greg's advocacy would surely offend many blacks today who wouldn't want to be patronized by an especially pale white guy. But he lived in a different time and his fierce beliefs, naive in many respects but often closely reasoned with little peer or other external influences, were quite remarkable for a young man destined to die in his very early 20s.

Jerry, Jim and I along with several others were Greg's apolitical, drinking friends. Beyond us, he had another circle, not so much friends as political and academic associates. This little band of university gypsies were the people he worked with during elections, protests and any other mischief that occurred to their contrary intellects. They were mostly a scraggly bunch who disagreed with each other about almost everything except their contempt for authority, and who were destined through maturation and financial necessity to wind up with families and nondescript white-collar jobs. They were a little goofy, I thought, and their ideas were somewhere beyond left field, but I grudgingly admired their persistence in confronting odds that were invariably overwhelming. These determined young men and women were never to my knowledge on the winning side in an election or ever succeeded in gaining a single major objective. The struggle may have been more important to some of them than the final result. At the time, most students - particularly the military veterans who filled the nation's colleges and universities - were mainly and understandably interested in getting degrees for purely practical reasons. They were tired of shellfire and other explosives, and just wanted a good job and a new car.

I assumed that Greg's objective was to do some kind of field work in Anthropology, although it was likely there was also the prospect of teaching on a university level in his plans. His closer friends knew he intended to work toward a doctorate. We never discussed careers, possibly because most of us were enrolled in an institution called The College of Arts and Sciences and had no specific vision of future work. But drinking together certainly generated conversation on a spotty range of other subjects. We occasionally discussed religion, a practice Greg dismissed as "simply unacceptable." A fallen-away Roman Catholic for some reason he never disclosed or I don't remember, he distrusted not only religions but religious people, he told me, because "they usually had other equally illogical and destructive notions." He reserved his strongest invective, something bordering on vituperation, for those who held religious convictions they tried to foist onto others. He hated these proselytizers in the way Jews hate Hitler. Greg was only a little less distrustful of the United States Congress, major corporations and any politician who wasn't far enough left to justify a fat FBI file and an occasional wire tap.

Greg's mother died when he was very young and he lived during his formative years with an aunt who had two children of her own. One of his cousins, Bob, was a couple of years older than Greg and the other, Marilyn or Mimi, was younger. As Greg grew up in St. Louis, his father lived distantly in Chicago, barely part of his son's life. He apparently made financial contributions to Greg's support, but for some reason, perhaps known to the family, failed to make the full paternal connection.

I had the impression that Bob, given his seniority, had considerable influence on his younger cousin. That influence had little to do with Greg's political or social outlook but, rather, his sexual opinions and his willingness to express them openly to almost anyone, any time. He said he'd die to defend his right to masturbate, a position his friends thought sensible given our conviction he'd not soon find a young woman - or a woman of any age, for that matter - willing to put up with his scruffy language and rampant hominess. Once, during his high school years, he lay naked in bed one Saturday morning until the family's once-a-week maid entered the room and discovered him under a top sheet that resembled a miniature circus tent. She immediately understood a teenage erection was supporting the sheet, and told him to run some cold water on it before she reported the matter to his aunt.

Greg apparently loved his aunt with the same intensity he would have directed to his mother had he known her, but I only surmise that affection from shards of evidence because he wasn't one to openly express those kinds of feelings. Bob told me that Greg, when he was 15, came home past the household curfew, reeking of beer, and was confronted by his aunt, who didn't immediately recognize that he was quite drunk. "Gregory," she said to him, using his full name in that ominous way parents do when they're provoked, "you promised me you'd be home on time, and you wouldn't drink, Your word is worthless, and it's clear that you simply don't love me." He looked at her - this generally foul-mouthed kid who had never so much as said "damn" in her presence - and remorseful tears welled up in his eyes. "Of course I love you," he replied. "You're my fucking aunt, for Christ's sake."

As Greg and his cousin, Bob, progressed through puberty, Mimi, younger than both of them, learned early to avoid household corners, cul de sacs and other places of possible entrapment where her overheated brother and cousin might snag cheap feels on her developing body. They weren't apparently much of a threat, and Mimi survived these inconveniences with genuine affection for both Bob and Greg who, where outsiders were concerned, were very protective of her. She was, I think, mostly amused by their sexual clumsiness while we, Greg's friends, marveled at her tolerance.

We all reached 16 in 1945, which was the year the war ended with the German unconditional surrender in May at General Eisenhower's headquarters in France followed in early September when General MacArthur accepted the Japanese capitulation aboard the USS Missouri in Tokyo Bay. Unaware that as many as 55 million people, military and civilian, may have died in the war, and unlikely to have conducted himself differently had he known, Greg's serious thoughts were beginning to focus on racial injustice and other domestic social issues. For him, the war was distant and impersonal, unlike the intolerance toward blacks that was plainly visible in the exclusionary laws and practices he saw every day in St. Louis. It wasn't the deep south where blacks were not only denied fundamental civil and human rights and were too often confronted with physical abuse, but it was a deeply segregated city in every important respect. There was no public accommodations law and most restaurants, hotels, theaters and other common gathering places, not to mention decent jobs and housing, were not available to a significant minority of the population. Greg noticed these conditions, which now seem impossible not to notice, although at the time there were few whites in St. Louis or elsewhere in America who saw the paradox of our national myth - liberty and justice for all - played out against a history of first slavery, and later, social oppression. "If I was black," Greg once said, "I'd be so goddamn mad I'd get a gun and shoot every white son-of-a-bitch I could find." I was, of course, glad he was white.

Greg said he began seriously thinking about the race issue when a young black man he met told him he'd never been to one of the restaurants in the city's largest drive-in chain. He'd not only never had one of their locally famous hamburgers or milk shakes, he'd never heard of the chain or noticed their ubiquitous, over-lighted, over-rated, over-utilized bastions of fried ugliness. And he'd never heard of the chain, Greg realized, because they didn't operate anywhere near his neighborhood and he wasn't allowed to operate in the white areas of town. It was the deprivation of hamburger that first made him think there was something wrong in the land of the free and the home of the brave.

Despite a persistent streak of seriousness, Greg was a fun-loving sort who appreciated mischief, particularly if some ingenuity was attached to it. In the summer between the German and Japanese surrenders, the war-time liquor shortage coupled with the restrictions on liquor sales to minors inspired him to devise a plan that would allow us, including Jerry, Bob and me, to gather a good supply of free liquor. All we had to do, he explained, was spend an evening aboard The Admiral, a large excursion boat that operated up and down the Mississippi River from its dock on the St. Louis waterfront. Greg had noticed on previous excursions that some passengers who brought their own liquor aboard and purchased mixers and food from the wait staff often got tanked or something near it and left their half-full bottles behind in the rush to get off the boat at the end of the evening. The plan was to swiftly collect those bottles as the tables emptied, and to cart the liquor off in common brown paper bags.

In theory, the plan seemed flawless, but Greg had failed to factor in a vital consideration, as we learned to our consternation one balmy summer night as The Admiral was being tied to its dock and hundreds of half-stewed passengers were pushing, shoving and stumbling their ways to and across the gangplanks that led to the old brick levee and dry land. The four of us, stationed at strategic positions as the boat approached shore, had descended on our assigned tables with what we originally thought was withering promptness until we realized the waiters had beaten us to every bottle worth having. The liquor had disappeared like objects in a magic show and we were left holding our paper bags. Later, we weren't amused when Greg told us we'd learned a valuable lesson from the experience. "The race," he said, "does, indeed, go to the swiftest" So does the booze, I probably thought.

OCHO

I saw my first bullfight one afternoon during that week we spent in Mexico City. Unfortunately, it was summer, not the season when the principal matadors and the bravest bulls are pitted against one another to demonstrate, I suppose, that there's more to life than romance. I had tried to persuade Laura and Mary Beth to go with me, but they had other plans which they made, I suspect, immediately after my invitation. I subsequently asked others from the workshop group and got the same response until my invitation to Jack Doby was overheard by the Misses Jamison and Cooper, who apologized for eavesdropping and inquired if they could "tag along." They could and did.

I knew little about the sport other than the information I'd gathered from Hemingway, particularly his "Death in the Afternoon." I felt and still feel about bullfighting much the same way I feel about hunting. I don't fight bulls and I don't shoot other animals for sport, but I don't knock it. I don't know any bullfighters, but I've known many hunters and most of them were reasonably decent relatively humane people who occasionally killed birds and certain mammals just as their ancestors had before them. The main difference, of course, was that their killing equipment was a good deal more efficient than the devices available in ancestral times and they usually had ample food at home in their refrigerators. But if your kind is at the top of the food chain, there are those who need to prove it from time to time. Miss Jamison and Miss Cooper, I soon learned, seemed to understand this fundamental truth.

The matadors we saw that day were of a lesser ilk than the ones who fought in the winter season, although one of them had a certain dogged tenacity that won my respect despite his ham-handed and bloody clumsiness, and the animals didn't seem particularly anxious to participate in an activity that, they seemed to sense, could only lead to trouble. These bulls came from a more prudent strain than the ones who wrung oles from the winter crowds, but the final result was almost always the same for both kinds.

The spectacle - made up of the richly colored sights, surging Spanish sounds and unfamiliar smells - was, as someone once said, worth the price of admission. I got the impression I was among Mexicans whose lives had nothing to do with tourism and who were there solely for their own amusement. My companions seemed to enjoy themselves, chatting amiably to each other as they had probably done for more than 50 years and largely ignoring me with the exception of an occasional question or request. I noticed for the first time that the two ladies could have been twins. They both had mainly white hair, almost the same shade, tied back in those buns older women, including both of my grandmothers, used to wear. They both had diaphanous skin, very finely lined, and they both wore delicate, wire spectacles. Their voices were low and gentle, and their movements, although slowed by age, were still purposeful. They made their way without any assistance from me, as they had probably made their way without any assistance from anyone else throughout their lives. I never learned their first names because my use of them, given the shortness of our acquaintance and our age differences, would have been, for them, an unendurable audacity. They were, after all, Victorian ladies who had deeply penetrated the 20th century.

Given these characteristics, which were obvious to anyone who observed them for more than a few minutes, I was surprised to hear Miss Cooper whisper halfway through the third bullfight to Miss Jamison, "He's a clod, but the little chap has balls." We were watching the matador whose fundamental incompetence was only surpassed by his persistence and courage. At great danger to himself he was making a bloody mess of the poor animal. And Miss Cooper - not by accident I'd guess - had selected the time-honored way to describe male Spanish courage.

Both women had taught in the same public school system in upstate New York, and had retired in the early 1930s after more than 40 years before the blackboards. They had chided enough urchins in their days to populate a small Balkan nation, and their educational careers had begun before the turn of the 20th century. One was a couple of years older than the other, but both had been born shortly after the end of the American civil war.

I made these and other more Intimate discoveries about the Misses Jamison and Cooper in the course of a few social drinks we had together in the hotel bar later that day. I'd asked them to join mc for a nip, expecting a polite refusal but getting, instead, a quietly enthusiastic acceptance from both women. They had a thirst, it turned out, that they'd cultivated over the years. And while their capacities were relatively small, they sipped their cocktails - gin martinis, straight up - with what I can only describe as relish. Miss Jamison, I recall, delicately smacked her lips after each sip as if to say, "Delicious."

I had not yet learned to sip my drinks and before long we were all in a conversational mood. We initially discussed the bullfights but soon drifted into more personal territory. The ladies, I found, knew a good deal more about bullfighting than I did because they'd been to Spain several times and seen the real thing. They also seemed to know a good deal more about bullfighters than I would have expected, which made me think there was more to their stories than they were likely to reveal. They were, as you might suspect, circumspect by nature, but they were also a couple of conspiratorial old girls not above putting me on for the pure fun of it. Miss Cooper told me about one bullfighter in particular - describing him in such vivid detail, both physically and psychologically - that I knew he'd been more than a passing acquaintance. Her recollections were so detailed it was difficult to realize she was talking about someone she had known more than 50 years earlier. I tried to imagine her as a young woman passionately engaged with a Spaniard who fought bulls, but the image wouldn't come.

They spoke of western Europe before the First World War, evoking an image of a historical period they had witnessed and I only knew indirectly from books I'd read. It was an era that had been destroyed by the violence and negative force of that great conflict and the national animosities that continued into the 1920s and 1930s, finally producing an even more brutal episode we unimaginatively called World War II. But the ladies remembered the good, middle-class hotels and what they construed as the pervasive refinement of the years before 1914 when the first war broke out. I could almost hear a waltz being played by some Viennese orchestra as they kept reminding each other of one vacation incident after another in one European country after another many years earlier. They seemed to have total recall, making references to particular dresses they'd worn or dinners they'd enjoyed on summer evenings in Italy before Theodore Roosevelt was president of the United States. The world of their youth was quite different than mine at the mid-point of the 20th century and the one that would evolve in the ensuing decades. A young school teacher I briefly knew, Jane McCabe, was vacationing a few years later in Italy, where she met and, I suppose, romanced an Italian military aviator. She later told me they were walking one morning along a major Roman thoroughfare when he asked if he could kiss her foot. " Not on your sweet life," was her first response, but he was persistent and she eventually relented. "What the hell," she thought or that's what she told me she thought. The flyer went down on one knee, grasp her foot in both hands and, as he kissed it, swiped his cheek on her bristly leg, which she'd neglected to shave that day. He looked up at her, momentarily startled, but made the perfect Italian recovery. "Every rose has its thorn," he said.

There was no public foot kissing on the streets of Rome when the Misses Jamison and Cooper were young. I was beginning to think their travels were mainly those typical spinster journeys that school teachers made in those days until one of them -Miss Jamison, I think - casually referred to the Riff rebellion in North Africa, which apparently broke out when they were in Morocco during the early 1920s. She implied they had met Abd el-Krim, a name I had never before suspected, let alone heard, but who, she patiently explained, was a Berber leader who organized resistance to Spain in what was then Spanish Morocco and through a decisive military victory drove the bastards out of the country. He subsequently formed a republic and served as its president until 1926 when his forces were defeated by a large Franco-Spanish army under command of Marshall Philippe Petain, who had been commander in chief of the French armies in the first world war.

She had aroused my curiosity and I wanted to know more about the Moroccan rebellion and their related personal experiences, but I was out of luck. They had turned their attention to "poor Marshall Petain" whose brilliant military career had been bitterly overshadowed by his service as premier of the Fascist-dominated Vichy government in unoccupied France from the French defeat by the Germans in 1940 to 1944. The Marshall was convicted in 1945 of collaboration with the enemy and sentenced to death, a sentence that was commuted to life imprisonment by French president Charles De Gaulle, another military hero. Since Petain was almost 90 at the time, you'd think the humiliation would have killed him in any event. But the arrogant, old geezer lived on for another five or six years, probably to prove that a Marshall of France can go the distance. Or, perhaps, for no reason at all.

The two women talked on, stimulated by the gin, no doubt, and provided several other indications that their summer travels had intersected with history from time to time. But I'd learned my lesson with Abd el-Krim and his rebellion, and I wasn't going to fall into that trap again. I politely and patiently listened to the ladies as they sipped their way slowly through two martinis apiece, thanked me for the afternoon, and left our table in the bar, bound, I thought, for their room and a couple of good naps.

NINE

For several years after my father's death in 1938 I spent my summers with his parents in the small Arkansas town where he had lived most of his short life. My mother, immediately after each school year ended, would put me on a Missouri Pacific Railroad train, no doubt heaving a great sigh of relief as I was trundled off for the seven hour trip to Memphis and an invariable meeting with my father's younger and only brother, Jack. From there, we'd drive the 50 miles, crossing the old Mississippi River Bridge and the Tennessee-Arkansas line, to the community where my dad had lived and died.

The train trip - which I first made alone when I was seven years old - was always an adventure. I was given a little pocket money and, it seemed, complete freedom to do as I pleased for the better part of a waking day. I was, of course, under loose supervision by the railroad conductors, who in those days took what was probably an unofficial responsibility for children traveling alone. Those tall men in dark blue uniforms owned gold pocket watches they seemingly examined at precise intervals. I remember one conductor who impressed me tremendously when he carefully noted that his watch was off by some fraction of a second. The train, we both failed to notice, was an hour and a half late.

The observation and dining cars on those trains were elegant, although that word was not in my vocabulary at the time. I usually ate lunch in the dining car, where someone made certain I was seated with an elderly, male stranger who didn't mind the company of children. I recall these strangers, usually grandparental types, treated me with the respect due a fellow traveler. They spoke to me as if I were a real person and not something with the intellect of a smart dog. I enjoyed those lunches with equals and everything else about the trains except the cost of things, which seemed prohibitively expensive to me. They charged 25 cents for a Coca Cola when the standard price everywhere else was a nickel. This experience instilled in me a life-long distrust of transportation companies, including those that operate anything from airplanes to river boats.

The uncle who met me in Memphis was a friendly, masculine man with one incredibly bad habit. He always greeted me with a kiss on the lips, perhaps a family or southern trait, but an intimacy, never-the-less, that I seldom allowed my mother. The prospect of that kiss, which I knew was coming, always set me on edge for the last hour of the train trip.

I spent many of my childhood summers in that little Arkansas town and my first few days were always marked by a profound insomnia induced by the deafening sound of country silence unbroken by the streetcars and buses that passed our St. Louis apartment building at regular intervals throughout the night. There were only those infernal crickets, billions of them, I would have guessed, rubbing something together or whatever they did to keep me awake. As you might expect in this goofy world, I gradually acclimated to the rural sounds, eventually found them soothing and was especially disturbed by the nocturnal streetcars - boxy, yellow machines that loudly clanged along, no matter the hour - when I returned to the city at the end of those summers.

I enjoyed the vacations when I was very young and also for the first few years after my father's death when I was moving from about 10 to 13 years old. On the days it didn't rain, I'd go to the well-kept, little public swimming pool at one edge of town or roam the countryside with a few friends I'd made for the summer. We'd haunt the area where a Civil War battle, not large by historical standards, had been fought, looking for and occasionally finding fragments of shot molds used in the conflict. Once we discovered an old, shored-up embankment along the small, meandering creek where the battle had raged, and we were sure we'd found what had been a cannon emplacement. We didn't know the battle had only been a bloody skirmish, a deadly little encounter between Union cavalry and southern raiders without artillery on either side, and that the embankment had been roughly constructed years later as part of a picnic grounds that was never completed

My grandfather sometimes took me swimming on hot evenings when the public pool had been refilled with frigid spring water from a town well. He'd usually say something about the medicinal qualities of really fresh, cold water until he felt a warm pocket, real or imagined, that convinced him some irresponsible oaf or child had peed in the pool. "Time to go," he'd say, and we'd head for the showers.

My grandfather was a self-made man, a splendid example, by his own admission, of unskilled labor. He was something between a horse tractor without the horses and an entrepreneur, owning a farm implement dealership as well as a tire store, and running a number of other legitimate enterprises I never quite understood. He'd been industrious as a young man, I'd been told, but I never saw him do anything that resembled work. He preferred to play Pinochle in the back of his tire store with several old cronies, and leave the businesses to Jack and, when he lived, my father. One of my grandfather's Pinochle-playing friends, Mr. Benstead, was a huge man who regularly sat on a small barrel, his vast ass overlapping that improvised chair like the Mississippi River overflowing its banks in flood. I don't remember his other friends, perhaps because they were usually obscured behind Mr. Benstead. These men played cards and drank whisky every afternoon, except Sunday when the store was closed. I never' saw my grandfather drunk, but there were apparently times when he slipped over the line from absolute sobriety. In the evenings, he often made the short drive out of town to inspect a few of his warehouses and make certain his hired watchman was awake. Armed with a .38, he sometimes drove along those country roads firing out the car window at rabbits in the passing fields. That was a sure sign he'd been drinking, my uncle told me when I was older, because there weren't any rabbits, at least none he would have seen from the car.

Short and robust, even into early old age, my grandfather was an exceedingly tidy man. His short, gray hair was parted precisely in the middle and in the summer he wore neatly pressed seersucker pants, either blue or gray, and either white or pale blue short-sleeved shirts. I must have seen the man at other seasons, but I only remember him in seersucker pants and short-sleeved shirts. For all I know, he could have worn reindeer hides and mukluks in the winter.

My grandmother was small, quiet and, it seemed to me, often amused in a detached way. I was her first and oldest grandchild and, eventually, the son of her dead first-born child. Given this special status, she was especially tolerant of me as I reached 13 and suddenly became a more difficult summer guest. By that, I only mean I was a typical teenage pain in the ass.

I had reached an age where I was intrigued by sex, but didn't quite understand what it was. I had also begun to distain the quiet small town, devoid of my friends back home and, I thought, any semblance of civilized life. Those bloody night-time crickets, too, began to really piss me off. For those and other reasons too tedious to mention, my 13th year included the last summer I spent in Arkansas.

That summer - which was less than six months before the Japanese bombed Pearl Harbor and the country went to war - I had opportunities to get into enough mischief to satisfy any reasonable teenager, which is surely an oxymoron if I've ever heard one. My grandparents went to bed early and left their doors unlocked, a common practice before television kept people awake and robbers made it prudent to padlock everything worth more than a dime. Given those conditions, I would stay out until two or three in the morning with a new friend and tell my grandmother the next day I had gotten in a little after nine.

The friend was a young man my age, John Morehouse, who was living temporarily with his grandmother, who also retired early and left her doors unlocked. His father was a career naval officer, on duty somewhere far from Arkansas, and his mother, I believe, had died a few years earlier. Together, John and I took power in the town once the adults had gone to bed and most of the lights were off. We wandered the streets on foot, stealing green pears from trees in the yards of neighbors who would have gladly given us the fruit had we asked, and throwing the half-eaten remnants into the two or three privately-owned swimming pools in the community. We threw stones at the infrequent street lights, fixed near the tops of high wooden poles, and occasionally broke one, just to watch the exploding bulb and blaze of white light before the area joined the profound darkness around it. And usually about mid-night we'd go to the ice plant, where we had stored a watermelon earlier in the day among other melons whose owners had scratched their family names into the rinds, either for ready identification or to make it easier for John and I to do something really stupid. One night, we spotted a particularly plump melon that belonged to the family of a girl we knew, one of the nicest, friendliest young virgins in the county. Her outstanding and obvious virtue, I think, practically drove us to carve "Mary," which was her name, "is a slut" into the dark green rind.

Once, my grandfather let us use his pick-up truck, unwilling to trust the family sedan to someone who'd been driving for less than a month, and instructed me to remain in town, drive slowly and get home early. Naturally, John and I immediately headed for the highway where we could push the old heap to its limits. We drove to several nearby towns, explored the unpaved back-roads that crisscrossed the countryside until the gasoline gauge approached empty, and then took the truck home. My grandfather gave me hell the next day, telling me I wouldn't get another chance to drive that summer because I'd been on the highway against his explicit instructions to stay in town. I recall we were standing in the drive-way next to the truck when I asked him how he knew we'd been on the road. He looked at me as if he were peering over spectacles, which he didn't wear, and pointed at the windshield and headlamps, which were heavily encrusted with dead bugs. Those innocent insects had obviously been flattened by speeds that would have been untenable inside the city limits. Clarence Darrow couldn't have gotten me out of that one.

There were fundamentalist religious revivals in the small, treeless park across the street from my grandparent's house that summer. Held early on warm nights, the meetings attracted surprisingly large crowds, many of the people drawn from the surrounding farmland by religious zeal or, perhaps, the need to socialize. They were exclusively poor whites, which during the latter years of The Depression meant they were really poor. Most of them would have had to inherit money to reach the poverty level. But they listened intently to those preachers, whose strong, resonant voices easily reached, without electrical amplification, the back rows, and responded with amens and other appropriate words of corroboration. Sitting across the street on my grandparent's porch steps, I couldn't hear the exact words, but the message somehow got through in the rhythmic give and take of the preachers and their audiences.

The revival crowds were only surpassed by those on Saturdays when the small downtown area teemed with country people, black and white, who had come, mainly on mule-drawn, flat-bed wagons, to buy, sell or trade something or just to loaf around one of the two drug stores or the five-and-dime. The men mainly wore clean coveralls, often faded from indigo to near white, and most of them chewed tobacco when they could afford it. The streets and walks were awash in tobacco juice, and you had to step carefully to avoid those large, obnoxious quids that stippled the thoroughfares. The mules, too, had left their mark on the streets, maybe a protest against the hardness of their lives.

The final summer, distinguished as it was by one petty offense on my part after another, eventually petered out, as seasons usually do. My grandparents, with the exception of the bug-battered truck, were unaware of my crimes and I returned without further reprimand or any punishment to St. Louis at the end of August. I never saw John again, and didn't get back to Arkansas until five years later when my grandfather died and I was given special leave from the Marine Corps to attend his funeral. My last trip to the ancestral home, five years later still, was to attend my grandmother's funeral, which was conducted on an intensely hot and humid July day shortly after I was married and just before I returned to Columbia to resume my quest for a university degree, any degree. Dressed in my only suit - an old, gray flannel number - I damn near died of heatstroke at my grandmother's graveside, an experience that taught me to avoid funerals and plan for my own cremation.

My mother's relations with my father's parents had soured after her divorce and some of her feelings toward them, not bitter but hardly amicable, had been subliminally transferred to me. I continued to love them, but in a qualified and not very affectionate manner, a cold fact I came to regret in my maturity. It's comforting to have warm feelings toward your closer relatives, but there's also no point in crying over spilt grandparents.

DIEZ

At the end of the week in Mexico City, I drove to Taxco down the old Pan American Highway with Laura and her cousin, Mary Beth. The two women who made the trip to Mexico with me traveled the final leg to Taxco by motor coach with the rest of the workshop people.

On our final evening in Mexico City, I had gone to the hotel registration desk to check for messages and found, instead, Juan Callahan, who managed the establishment and had spelled the desk clerk for his dinner period. Since there were no other guests in the small lobby and Senor Callahan had no real work to accomplish until the clerk returned, we drifted into a conversation that became more extended than either one of us would have expected. I learned almost immediately that Callahan, a Mexican national with some obvious genetic disposition toward Ireland, had recently returned to his native country from Switzerland, where he had worked for and ultimately managed a small hotel in Zurich. He was fluent, I soon discovered, in English, French, German, Italian and, naturally, Spanish, and he had seen everything in western Europe worth seeing before a good deal of it got trashed in the recent war. A man of formal habits, probably in his mid-50s, Mr. Callahan politely inquired about my purpose in Mexico and my general interests. We were, by the time the clerk returned, engaged in conversation to the extent he, Callahan, invited me into his office just off the lobby for a drink before I went off to meet friends for dinner. I accepted the invitation and wound up with a single malt scotch several years before my body and mind became acclimated to that splendid beverage. As we sat there sipping our drinks, he told me he had served as an intelligence agent for "the Americans" during the war years, using his position at the Swiss hotel as a cover. His sympathies, he said, were largely neutral, but we, meaning the Americans, paid well for his services and wartime conditions were difficult, even in a non-belligerent nation like Switzerland. I didn't know if he was telling the truth or lying like the spy he never was, but the story was interesting and he also told me in very general terms a good deal about Mexican history and culture. He seemed to take pride in both the ancient native achievements - vast building projects and other evidence of developed societies - as well as the Spanish conquest and subsequent dominion over the country. I attributed this apparent contradiction to his dual ancestry, which I simply presumed based on his family name. He had predecessors on both sides of the Atlantic.

We probably spent no more than an hour together, Mr. Callahan and I, before his work and my obligation to meet Laura and Mary Beth forced a conclusion to our conversation. Looking back, I was surprised at the amount of information, personal and general, the man had dispensed in that short time period. I wondered then and I still occasionally wonder if he talked to others as openly as he talked to me that evening and, if not, why I got elected. I knew even then that it wasn't my erudition or cultured manner, let alone magnetic personality or any other singular trait that separated me from the rest of those who passed through Mr. Callahan's hotels. Did he just need a thought purgative that evening and a live body to justify it or was he trying to tell me something for a specific reason? Or was he just lonely? Those questions are the kind that never get answered. It's the accumulation of those kinds of questions that drive some people to religion.

Laura, Mary Beth and I left Mexico City on a sunny June morning and lunched in Cuernavaca, a town with pastel houses, red-tiled roofs and an abundance of brilliant flowers and vibrant vegetation. It wasn't difficult to understand why the area had long been a popular summer retreat for the powerful and wealthy from the nearby capital, including Aztec emperors and the Spaniard, Hernando Cortes, who conquered Mexico in the 16th century. With a handful of men and a few horses, he not only destroyed an Aztec empire but set the tone for colonial suppression that would endure in the region for 300 years. He left a cruel legacy, but he lived in cruel times.

Between 1504 when at 19 he first sailed from Spain to Santo Domingo in the new world and November 8, 1519 when he and his troops entered the Aztec capital of Tenochtitlan, now Mexico City, and took the emperor Montezuma hostage, Cortes had risen to command important discovery and military expeditions in the region. He subsequently fought and defeated other Spaniards sent to arrest him as well as the Aztecs, who rebelled after Montezuma's death and evicted Cortes and his men from their city in a dramatic and bloody battle with a melodramatic Spanish name, la noche triste, which essentially means the Spaniards got their butts kicked.

Not easily discouraged, Cortes regrouped and with native allies defeated the Aztecs once and for all. He went on to become the colonial governor, but was deposed by his political enemies and recalled to Spain in 1528. But the following year he was granted honors by Charles V and confirmed as Captain General of New Spain, a title, I presume, with sufficient grandiosity for almost any Spaniard of that time. He returned to Mexico in 1530 and discovered lower California in 1536, although, like most geographical discoveries and as someone else once observed, the inhabitants probably knew where they were all along. Cortes again returned to Spain in 1540, managed later to get shipwrecked on an expedition to Algiers and - probably his most surprising achievement - died, I gather, with his boots off, at home on his estate near Seville. He was 62, not a bad run for someone with his penchant for dangerous military and political activities.

Cortes' conquest of Mexico was as daring and unlikely to achieve success as it was relentlessly cruel in both its immediate and long-term results. The Spaniards in Mexico and elsewhere in the western hemisphere managed to enslave or eradicate whole cultures, and they did it with missionary zeal and pious rationalizations as many of them sought to enrich themselves and their sovereigns. Those motives were generally prevalent in Mexico during the conquest, but the story is never-the-less a splendid adventure unmatched in fiction, with few exceptions, and told superbly in one of my favorite books. Written by William H. Prescott, who died before the American civil war began, the "History of the Conquest of Mexico" is for me an extraordinary account of an almost impossible achievement. A blind man who had never been to Mexico or Spain where the important archival material, usually essential to any competent historian, was stored, Prescott managed to get that information by other means, and also wrote, among other things, a history of the conquest of Peru, carried out by another Spaniard with more courage, cruelty and greed than ordinary good sense, even for the period and place. This one, Francisco Pizarro, brought down a powerful Inca empire.

Incidental to the grand story, an Aztec princess the Spaniards called Marina or Malinche was given to Cortes as a slave but became his mistress and interpreter, and helped him in other ways during the conquest of Mexico. She eventually married a soldier, Juan de Jaramillo, and with him went to Spain.

Malinche reminds me of Sacagawea, the Shoshone Indian woman who served as an interpreter on the Lewis and Clark expedition that revealed a good part of the American west to eastern minds in the early 1800s. She, too, had been enslaved and through intelligence, pluck and other good qualities probably contributed as much as anyone to the safe completion of a rather important historical project. And she, too, seemed to like the strangers who would eventually destroy her native culture.

We lunched leisurely at one of the hotel restaurants, scarcely aware in that serene, flower-filled environment of the bloody history of the conquest hundreds of years earlier, and completely unaware that Cuernavaca had been a battleground only 40 years before that pleasant June day in 1950. There's an ancient pyramid -probably erected by the Aztecs - that was discovered in 1910 during the Mexican Revolution when a large hill on the outskirts of Cuernavaca was used as a gun platform for shelling the city. The rumbling gunfire displaced some of the soil covering the buried pyramid, proving once and for all that war sometimes has its useful side.

We ate our lunches in historical ignorance, discussing events of the past week, and then drove the remaining distance to Taxco. We arrived that afternoon and checked in at the Hotel de la Borda before moving the next day to the Casa Humboldt. I inadvertently locked my keys in the car shortly after our arrival, and the hotel manager, equipped with a metal ring loaded with automobile keys, found one within minutes that fit my door lock. He opened the door with a subtle smugness that made me determine never to repeat that particular mistake. I went the following morning to one of the silver shops endemic to Taxco and had my combination door and ignition key put on a light chain to wear around my neck. I reasoned that the key was safe unless I lost my neck, in which case the importance of a locked car door would be considerably diminished. One of a half dozen young silver smiths in the small shop fitted by General Motors key to an appropriate chain, which seemed to amuse all of them. They whispered to each other in Spanish, casting occasional glances in my direction. It was only later that I realized the faithful - particularly in heavily Roman Catholic countries such as Mexico - were more likely to dangle religious medals than corporate logos from their necks. But I wore that key all summer and it had all the properties of a good talisman. I not only didn't lock myself out of the car again, I didn't care as long as I felt that key reassuringly nestled against my chest.

ELEVEN

Laura was the only child of wealthy parents who brought their daughter up to understand her position in a privileged society. She understood it, I'm sure, and accepted its comforts, but the people who came to interest her as she matured were not generally the business and professional men and their wives who populated the old country club and who were the occupants of Laura's social world. She maintained over the years her contacts with many of them, including a few she considered close friends, although her more intimate associates were increasingly drawn from the art and academic communities, at first in Dallas and, as she began to travel more widely, from cities around the country and, later, countries around the world. From early on, she sought experiences that contributed to an expanding sophistication, but she retained an exterior softness and amiability that artfully disguised an inner toughness and determination to live her life as she saw fit.

Her father, Sam Houston Bennett, was a native Texan and Harvard-educated attorney whose wealthy clients often doubled as social friends. They were the oil men, doctors and politicians, among others, who ran the city and state, and whose influence extended to New York, Washington and beyond. Maddie, Laura's mother, was originally an outlander whose Boston origins had long and successfully been submerged beneath a southern veneer. Both had been bred to a conservatism so fundamental it could have been genetically based. Sam and Maddie, no doubt, loved their bright, pretty daughter, but I had the distant impression distilled from a number of things Laura told me about them and her childhood that she thought their love was conditioned on her abilities and behavior. She was, she thought, a part of their lives in much the same way their stately Dallas home or ranch in west Texas comprised part of the Bennett holdings. Laura told me she wondered how she would have fared as a daughter had she been a Downs child or simply someone who was unable to carry her own social weight.

But she did carry that weight and decided early in life to keep her contrary opinions, infrequent as they were, to herself. It was a habit she carried over into her marriage to Stanley Chase, son of a prominent Dallas businessman and, like her father, a Harvard graduate. Unlike her father, he had not gone on to get a law degree from a Texas university but, rather, had returned home to work in the family enterprise, a manufacturing company he would control one day when his own father either died or tired of its management. Laura and Stanley's marriage, best described as placid, produced two daughters, and a mild disposition toward infidelity on her part once the early passion in their relationship had cooled. She had what she called her "initial affair" with a young naval officer when she and Stanley, also a young naval officer, were living in San Francisco during the war. There was apparently some discernible difference between young naval officers or, at least, she thought so at the time.

Although infrequent, there were other men in Laura's life from time to time, and they were, I gathered, little more than diversions from the constraints of social habits and obligations she would eventually discard. I, too, was one of those diversions, but for some odd reason she confided things in me I'm sure she didn't tell the others. She may have thought I was smart enough to know my youth and financial circumstances precluded any kind of permanent relationship with her. Or, more likely, she probably just felt like talking at the time, and I was non-threatening and handy.

I learned during one of our discussions that her best friend at the New Orleans school she attended was a young woman named Mary McCready, whose home was in the same small southern town where my father lived and died. To further compound the coincidence, my parents, shortly after their marriage, settled in the community and rented an old house I heard described in later years as "the McCready place," meaning that one of Mary McCready's relatives, perhaps her father or grandfather, had owned the house where my parents had first lived together and, more probably, where I was conceived. The revelation was a concept in its own right, but it didn't occur to me until much later that I originated in a house owned by a relative of Laura's best school friend. Small world, indeed.

Mary Beth came from a "poor" but respectable branch of the family on Laura's paternal side. I gathered that "poor" was a relative term among the Bennetts that would have meant middle class and comfortable to me and, I have no doubt, to Mary Beth as well. Also an only child, Mary Beth had attended public schools and graduated from one of the state universities to become a high school art teacher in the Dallas or a nearby school system. She had never married, although I noticed that men were often attracted to her, and she seemed to have little interest in more temporary unions, either with men or women, an attitude she conveyed clearly without quite saying so. I think she liked men well enough, but thought many of the ones she knew were dopes. Amiable dopes, usually, but dopes never-the-less. She had grown up in a small west Texas town, not far from the Bennett family ranch, and had moved to the Dallas area after her university graduation. The two cousins had known each other since girlhood, visiting back and forth when Laura spent summers on the ranch, and seeing each other with increasing frequency in Dallas after the war.

Laura and Mary Beth were surely drawn to each other by their mutual interest in art, but there was something more powerful in the attachment. They were so outwardly different in appearance, personality and temperament that the similarity that bound them together wasn't apparent, not even to them. They were both playful and conspiratorial - much like the Misses Jamison and Cooper - which allowed them to share those things they found mutually amusing as well as secrets that most others in their conservative worlds would neither understand nor approve. I didn't realize it at the time, but I later suspected that Laura more than likely revealed all the intimacies of our relationship to Mary Beth. I cringe to this day at the thought.

Laura's feelings about everything from her parents, husband and children to art and the world at large were often rendered with a flippancy that suggested those people and matters were only marginally important to her. The opposite was usually true, I think, and her manner was simply that device so many of us use to insulate ourselves from various vulnerabilities. In Laura's case, it served to disguise the real person who, she had decided early in life, was unsuitable for the social world in which she grew up. She had long since mastered that world when I met her, but well established habits are hard to break and there was little reason for her to change a personality that seemed to charm most of those she met, including me.

My impressions are, of course, nothing more than wild guesses, which may be enough to qualify me as a moderately accomplished psychoanalyst. I admit, then, that I really don't know much about Laura's true feelings, but it's reasonable to assume that painting was somewhere near the center of her life. I'm sure she loved her children and parents, despite certain ambivalences, and I think she was fond of her husband, infidelities aside, but she had a profound commitment to painting that may have run deeper than any of those familial attachments. And while Laura didn't resemble the popular concept of a committed artist, I think Mary Beth understood the depth of her cousin's commitment, respected it, and kept the knowledge to herself. And Laura reciprocated respect and, perhaps, an unconscious admiration for Mary Beth's talent and self-reliance. But, again, that's only a guess.

TWELVE

I had gotten into the Marine Corps on a two-year enlistment - an aberration for an organization that normally required a longer commitment - and I got out on schedule before my 20th birthday. Those two-year enlistments, as I told you earlier, were temporarily installed immediately after the Second World War to recruit more men and secure a larger appropriation for the Corps. Given the nation's historical and understandable affinity for post-war demobilizations, it was probably a sensible strategy that didn't quite work. When the Korean war broke out in 1950, the Corps and other military branches, judging by their need to call up partially trained reservists, were short of active manpower.

The Korean War was almost two years ahead on that warm, sunny day when I kissed the military goodbye forever, and left North Carolina bound for New York City with mustering out money and the determination to spend every cent of it before I went home to St. Louis. I was with my high school friend, Ed Kelly, who had also been discharged, and we had purchased a ride in a privately-owned automobile from the military base to Washington where we would take a train for the final leg of our trip to

New York. The ride we bought included three other paying passengers, also dischargees, and the driver, a wordless man whose main objective was to get us to Washington and get himself back to North Carolina as soon as possible to pick up another payload. It was a job that probably assured early eyesight problems as well as hemorrhoids.

Packed into that car like those smelly little fish in tin cans, I sat next to a window in the back seat and watched a continuous blur I assumed was the passing countryside as we sped toward the nation's capital. My only precise recollection of that trip was a sound - something like a rapidly dribbled basketball - that snapped me out of a semi-coma about halfway through the trip. "Flat tire" was my first thought until I looked out the rear window and saw chicken features swirling in our wake. I heard exactly the same sound two years later on the drive to Mexico City when I hit a scrawny bird who wandered into the path of my onrushing Chevrolet. It made me suspect there was something international, if not universal, about car-chicken collisions.

The train out of Washington was packed with soldiers, marines and a few sailors, most of them on leave from the various military installations down the Atlantic coast. Reminiscent of the war years, they filled all the seats and aisles, even the narrow passageway opposite the restroom compartments, one for men and another for woman, in our coach. Since we had not seen any women aboard, Ed and I along with two paratroopers from Ft. Bragg, North Carolina installed ourselves in the women's compartment, a cozy little two-room arrangement with comfortable seating separated from the toilet facilities. We had barely settled in for the trip when someone began banging loudly on the door with an insistence that demanded response. We thought it was the train conductor come to expel us from the premises but it was, instead, a soldier who spoke, he explained, for a young nursing mother who needed the privacy of the compartment to feed her hungry infant. We were, of course, suspicious, but the sound of an obviously distressed woman's voice on the other side of the door convinced us to relinquish our private quarters. The woman and her baby, probably refugees from another nearby coach, took over the compartment and we stood up the rest of the trip as that war-weary old train pitched and rolled up the coast.

We were delivered to Manhattan early that evening and took a cab from the train station to the Dixie Hotel, a busy but declining place near a Times Square that was just beginning its own descent. We checked in and went to our room, where we removed the woven gold discharge emblems - gold eagles we called "ruptured ducks" - from our uniforms. The emblems, we figured, made us natural marks for the thieves and con men who roamed the city. It told them we had mustering out pay.

We spent the next five days and our money in a near-frantic attempt to see a place that was essentially unseeable in a lifetime. We sought out not the Statue of Liberty or the Empire State Building, but the clubs on 52nd Street where a variety of jazz was sung and played by performers as diverse as Ella Fitzgerald and the boogie-woogie pianists, Ammonds and Johnson. We also cased a few of the night clubs, places like Leon and Eddie's where the entertainment was more lavish, drinks and everything else were more expensive and the audiences noisier and less appreciative than those in the jazz bars. Ed almost made himself sick at Leon and Eddie's, eating several bowls of nuts at the bar to compensate for the dollar and a quarter they'd charged him for a beer. That was big money to someone who'd just left an occupation that paid $75 a month.

I talked Ed into a visit to the Museum of Modern Art to see Picasso's "Guernica," that stark work inspired by the 1937 Fascist bombing of the ancient Basque town during the Spanish Civil War. Ed liked the painting - which years later was sent to Spain - but not as much as he liked Ella Fitzgerald or Ammonds and Johnson. His preferences were more auditory than graphic, but he had an open mind.

The high-water mark of our trip, probably, was a sheer coincidence made possible by a motherly ticket agent at the hotel. She sold us reasonably-priced tickets to "A Streetcar Named Desire" when it was difficult to get unreasonably priced ones at any price. The Tennessee Williams play, destined with its author to become theatrical institutions, was performed the night we saw it with Marlon Brando, Jessica Tandy, Karl Malden and Kim Hunter in principal roles. That was my first Broadway play and it had a considerable influence on me, at least for the short term. On my way to Europe several years later, I revisited Broadway to see another Williams play, "The Rose Tattoo," and still later saw most of the others, mostly in other places. I liked his stuff so much I managed to over-expose myself to his languid southern ladies and other strangeness and eventually grew sick of it. And isn't that a little lesson in life?

We took the mandatory subway rides, going nowhere in particular, strongly aware of our liberation from military bondage, and we walked mile after mile of

Manhattan pavement with the friendly knowledge we didn't have to be anywhere any time soon. On our last full day in New York, we met two young women - I don't remember where or how - who invited us to rent bicycles with them in Central Park. We rode until an unexpected but fortuitous rainstorm soaked us to our skins, evoking a second invitation, this time to the small apartment they shared somewhere downtown. We went there to dry out, but stayed until early the next morning, sustained by the spaghetti dinner they rustled up for us, cheap red wine and the expectation of more to come. The "more" we expected didn't come, fortunately, and it turned into a memorable evening unspoiled by what could have been a pedestrian one-night stand. One of the young women and I spent our final few hours together sitting on a couch in a dark room, an old record player providing musical accompaniment to softly falling spring rain outside a partly open nearby window. Ed and the other girl were in the kitchen, lights out and talking, as we were, in rambling generalities. Although I recall trivial details like the partly open window, I haven't the vaguest recollection of their faces, only the conviction these two young women were pretty and not yet old enough to vote. They were, I remember, from somewhere in Virginia where they were high school friends who decided to shuck their small town homes for the city. They both had to rise early the next day to work different but equally unskilled jobs, and we, too, had to get up early to go home. When we left them, the rain had stopped and we miraculously found an off-duty cab driver willing to take us back to the hotel only because he, too, had seen recent military service. Misery, sometimes, not only likes company but has its own rewards.

With little more than two hours sleep and not more than $20 each after we'd settled the hotel bill, Ed and I took a bus to the outskirts of somewhere and hitchhiked to another somewhere in Pennsylvania where we spent the night. The town was large enough to support a stock brokerage, an unusual way to measure population, perhaps, but one I remember because I wanted to check the market value of my Tucker Automobile securities. I'd bought 20 shares of Tucker common stock for about $100 on my last home military leave, and the value of that investment now pretty much represented my net worth, not counting the few crumpled bills in my pocket. The news at the brokerage house was not yet as bad as it would become before the company folded, victim, depending on who you believed, of an automotive industry conspiracy to ruin an audacious genius, Preston Tucker, or victim of the ultimate con man, Tucker himself. Personally, I always thought it was just another failed business venture with one distinction. It cost me $100.

I went on to invest money in a large brewery just before the Teamsters Union struck them for 18 months, effectively shutting down operations and decimating its stock price, and in an early mutual fund that was cited by the Securities and Exchange Commission or some organization of that ilk for mismanagement or worse. I put money into an airline that went belly up, and dribbled other small amounts into various ventures that would have needed improvement to become questionable. And I managed all that before I was 30 years old. These were, of course, hard financial lessons, but the experience enabled me to eventually forge a practical guide to money management that has governed my subsequent life. Distilled to its essence, that guide requires that you direct your income to three principal purposes. First, you pay your bills and, second, you save a little. Third and finally, you spend the rest in bars and restaurants. Call me loony, but there's a moral, practical and recreational balance to the plan that's unequivocal.

I didn't have any money to invest in anything as we hitched the remaining miles to St. Louis, eating an occasional hamburger or eggs in greasy little restaurants along the way. Some of those meals were paid for by truckers who'd given us rides, probably because our company and conversation not only passed the time but kept them from falling asleep on those long, monotonous hauls over beat up, two-lane roads. I learned that people who pick up hitchhikers will tell them things they wouldn't tell a spouse or a parent. Or a best friend. They'll sometimes dump a ton of emotional verbiage on a hitch-hiker because they know they'll never see that particular stranger again. Some of it, I thought, was a little weird, but it passed the time and did no detectable harm.

Our final ride into St. Louis took us to the Barrel Bar just as neatly as any commercial conveyance, only without the monetary exchange. The Barrel was a familiar hang-out, a place where I was likely to find someone who knew me well enough to justify a five dollar loan. I did and it was Gregory Upp, although our meeting was far less coincidental than you might suspect. There was no prearrangement, but Greg was in the bar, usually for a single beer, at least four or five times a week when he was in town from Columbia. He liked the music, and he knew the plain clothes cops who inspected the place from time to time wouldn't hassle anyone they thought was within a year or two of the legal drinking age. That evening, the music was supplied by a small group fronted by Jimmy Forest, who wrote and played his signature "Night Train" on a tenor or baritone saxophone whose honking sounds filled the small bar and spilled out onto Delmar Boulevard. One of the regular singers at The

Barrel, Ann Richardson - called Rock House Annie - was a tall, black woman who sang a thing called "The Chair Song" with a lyric that announced: "If I can't sell it, I'll sit on it. I ain't gonna give it away." The Rock House was an East St. Louis bar where she had performed for years before her Barrel period.

I don't remember our conversation, but I do recall - as we drank our beers at that long bar in that short building - a great sense of release, knowing that I didn't have to report back to a military base. We finished our drinks and I paid for them with some of the money Greg had loaned me, making certain I kept a nickel from the bar change for a telephone call I should have made earlier. We agreed to meet the next night for a drink, and I retrieved my small, canvas bag - just as Ed did - from the floor between our stools, and stopped at the public phone on our way out. I waved goodbye as they headed for the door, slotted the nickel, dialed the two letter exchange (Evergreen) followed by four digits, and waited for the rings to stop. It was only about eight thirty, but the woman who answered gave the impression the call had come in the middle of the night. "Hello," she said, almost reluctantly, "who is this?"

"It's me, mother," I replied. "I'm home." The sound of Jimmy Forest playing in the background made me think: "Well, not exactly."

TRECE

Taxco, one of the oldest mining towns in North America, provided gold for the early Spanish conquerors and later silver that enabled the French miner, Jose de la Borda, to amass an immense fortune in the 1700s. It was silver, in fact, that established the town's reputation, although its importance had waned by the time an American, William Spratling, arrived there in 1929. By then, I was told, the local silver artisans had died off and their skills were largely forgotten. Spratling, who left New Orleans to settle in Taxco, was instrumental in renewing the local silver crafts that attracted droves of tourists to the town once a proper highway was put through the rugged Sierre Madres. He was by 1950 something of a local legend, a wirey man with a deep tan who lived mainly alone in a villa filled with pre-Columbian artifacts and paintings by the principal Mexican revolutionary artists.

I met Spratling at a cocktail party he gave for our workshop group, primarily as a favor to his old friend, Janet Joslyn, and also, I suspect, to promote the town that had become an important part of his life. I had a long conversation with him that commenced when I asked about an incomprehensively dark painting on one of his walls. The painting had been made and given to him by either Jose Orozco or David Siqueiros, who with Diego Rivera were considered the Mexican nation's artistic triumvirate. The painter, Spratling explained, had mixed coffee grounds or some other destructible material with his paints to achieve a textural effect. The decomposing coffee had blackened the work, which Spratling had left on the wall, he said, as a demonstration of the artist's arrogance in assuming he could will a vegetable material to accomplish something only a mineral substance could do.

I also learned that Spratling and I shared an interest in aviation, and that he was a pilot who kept a small plane at a field near a place called Iguala south of Taxco. He had flown the aircraft - a two-place Aerocoupe - from Mexico to Alaska, and the journey had been covered by a popular aviation magazine. Spratling's description of the flight was overheard by Fred Newcomb, a young photographer I barely knew who was lodged at the Hotel de la Borda with most of the others in the workshop. He had been mingling with the guests - a drink in one hand, party food in the other - and by coincidence arrived within earshot as Spratling began to tell me about the flight to Alaska. Newcomb, too, was interested in airplanes and Spratling, in an act of considerable generosity, offered to fly us, one at a time in deference to the plane's capacity, over a major archeological excavation then underway in the region. His only stipulation was that we find our own way early the next morning to Iguala because he had other business later in the day and couldn't provide round-trip transportation from Taxco. Since I had a car and we were supposed to meet Spratling at the airfield about seven, I arranged to pick up Fred at six outside his hotel.

Punctual to a fault, I was there five minutes early, seated behind the steering wheel with my usual hangover and a genuine sense of expectation. "Buenos dias, senor," a voice, seemingly from nowhere, said. Startled, I did a 360 degree scan before I realized a boy was standing next to me outside the car. "Buenos dias," I replied. He was very small for his age, which I established at about 10 or 11 based on his manner. He was too assured for anyone younger or, at least, that was my assumption. I knew he was one of those little hustlers who volunteer to watch your parked car for a small fee. It's a fee you either pay or you can kiss your hubcaps goodbye. But he knew I wasn't going to park and he thought for a few moments, probably about his financial prospects with me, before he inquired: "You are from Mizz-zoor-ee, senor?" I realized he'd copped that information from my license plate, but I admitted that Mizz-zoor-ee was, indeed, my home. He thought for a minute and added: "I have many friends in Mizz-zoor-ee." That was probably a gambit of some kind, a stall to give him time to devise some fast money scheme. But Fred arrived, on time, and we left the boy with my silent best wishes for success in an enterprise that would have challenged a resourceful adult.

The morning sky was perfectly clear and the mountain air was nothing if not invigorating as we discovered the airfield was a short, grassy strip with a few old, wooden shacks that served as hangars. One of the buildings had a small, roof-top windsock, the only airport-like feature on the premises. Spratling had arrived ahead of us and his little, silver plane, glistening in the sharp morning light, was parked, engine idling, outside its shed. He wore a white dress shirt, open at the neck, buttoned at the wrists, and a pair of well-worn khaki trousers. We greeted one another, and he pointed at the Aerocoupe, an indication, I gathered, that he was ready to go. Given the plane's two-person capacity, including the pilot, Tom and I tossed a coin to see who got the first ride. I won.

The Aerocoupe climbed easily off the runway despite the thin mountain air. As we gained altitude, Spratling put the plane into a gentle bank and we began a long, upward spiral. From this new perspective, I understood the airport was a very small flat spot in the Sierre and the steepness of the surrounding terrain made it impossible to climb directly over those monumental impediments. Not in an Aerocoupe.

Once we gained sufficient altitude to clear one of the ridges, Spratling leveled the plane out and headed for our destination, a place, he told me, where archeologists sought the hidden burial ground of the last Aztec emperor, Cuauhtemoc. He had succeeded the wimp, Montezuma, and, despite eventual defeat, had redeemed native honor to some extent by inflicting a good beating on the Spanish before they collected themselves and sent the Aztecs into practical if not historical oblivion.

I have no recollection of the archeological site, probably because a camp is not much of a spectacle from several thousand feet up. But I remember the flight vividly and I recall Spratling smoking a cigarette and opening the canopy just enough to let the slipstream remove spent ashes from the butt. Seated next to him, I noticed as he closed the canopy an impressive chrome chronometer on his wrist, a heavy, multi-dialed instrument that told me he took his flying seriously.

Like many of the boys who grew up in the 1930s and either read or heard about a parade of pioneering flyers, I developed a strong interest in airplanes that might have led to a career in military aviation had my eyesight been keener. As it was, I just barely made it into the Marine Corps. But I early on built one model airplane after another, always powered by rubber bands because I never managed to save enough money to buy one of those tiny but relatively expensive gas-driven engines. I once convinced a friend we could build a real plane, using for power thousands of rubber bands harnessed to its propeller. The rubber bands, I reasoned, could be rewound in flight with a hand crank. The project never made it beyond the planning stage because my friend casually mentioned the idea to his father, who almost ruptured himself with laughter before he demolished the concept with adult certainties.

As a teenager, I usually had an after-school job during the week, but sometime during my 16th year I began working on weekends at a small airfield in the Illinois countryside. I got flight instruction instead of pay for those efforts and an opportunity to fly around in a variety of little airplanes that are now seen, if at all, at air shows and in museums. I eventually became a licensed pilot but a variety of distractions kept me from achieving the committed amateur status Spratling had attained. I've never flown a light plane to Alaska and I've never owned a serious chronometer. My plain wristwatch reveals me for the dodo I am.

I remember our landing when the Aerocoupe crested a mountain ridge, well below the peak, and we slipped neatly down a long, steep approach that put us in position to use all the limited runway space in that glorified pasture the locals called an airport. I never saw Spratling again and he wouldn't have known my name had someone blared it into his ear with a bullhorn, but I read his obituary in a forgotten publication when he died some years later. And I subsequently learned there is a Museo De Arqueologia Guillermo Spratling behind the Church of Santa Prisca in Taxco. The museum, I understand, contains pre-Columbian artifacts and paintings by various artists, which are probably those things that decorated his home.

Although Fred and I saw each other from time to time over the course of that summer, I don't think we exchanged more than a passing pleasantry. It wasn't that we didn't like one another, it was just that the distance between the Hotel de la Borda and the Casa Humboldt couldn't be measured with conventional instruments.

FOURTEEN

The weather in Columbia seemed especially cold during the last winter of Greg's life. I don't know whether the temperatures were any lower than usual or if our exposure to the elements was greater than ordinary. Jim Kelly and I shared an unheated room in a transplanted military barracks where the only warmth derived from a central study area served by a large oil heater. These barracks, renamed Student Housing to give them academic credibility and to accommodate the hordes of military veterans then enrolled at the University, covered a large tract of land near the football stadium. I figured our Spartan quarters were actually a subtle message from the authorities, a message that told us to watch our steps or they'd start another war and guess who'd be the first to go.

I slept that winter in sweat shirt, sweat pants and sweat socks under my heavy wool Marine Corps blanket, wishing each bone-numbing morning that I'd had enough sense to attend some school, any school, in Florida. I had appropriated the bottom bunk, which left thc upper one for Jim, whose knees - ruined by high school football - made it difficult for him to get out of that lofty bed on some days. There were occasions when I had to get someone from one of the other three bedrooms in our barracks to help me lift poor Kelly out of the sack. Those were the times his damaged knees locked on him and he could only bend at the waist and elbows. Once we got Jim on his feet, he could usually work his knees free, allowing him to dress, breakfast on a bag of Popcicles he kept on the sill outside our window, and toddle sorely off to class. Actually, he only ate Popcicles for breakfast toward the end of the month when his money ran low.

All the military veterans without family means seemed to run out of money at the end of the month. Our educations were financed by a marvelous Congressional gift we called the G.I. Bill, short for G.I. Bill of Rights, which paid our tuition and provided a modest monthly check to help with living expenses. Since that money was never meant to supply us with beer, it inevitably failed to last the full month. Jerry and I, put off by Popcicles on frosty winter mornings, preferred to breakfast on cheeseburgers and beer at The Stable, where we and a few chosen others were allowed to run tabs at an enterprise that was mainly a cash business. One of the others - a resourceful young man from a modestly affluent family that included a particularly naive mother - got his Stable bill on letterhead, which he sent home for payment. He told mom the expense was connected with horsemanship, which the G.I. Bill didn't cover. Jerry and I, once we'd received our monthly government checks and paid our tabs, began the new months with ever diminishing resources, which guaranteed we'd be back on the cheeseburger breakfasts earlier than ever. It was a strong lesson in money management that probably had some subliminal effect. Aside from early automobile loans and later home mortgages, we both avoided debt like the proverbial plague, which meant we'd never leverage our money and gain the potential for real wealth. I blame my loss of prospects on cheeseburgers.

Like our lesson in money management, Kelly, too, learned a strong lesson that winter. He left the University of Missouri at the end of the spring semester to attend a small college in Oakland, California where the weather made it easier for him to get out of bed in the morning. He had also learned to avoid top bunks and other places of likely entrapment for a young man with the worst knees outside professional football.

Jim was a red-haired, blue-eyed Irishman with a short, neatly trimmed beard who could affect one of those phony German accents that sounded as if it had come directly from some worn-out comedy routine. Once and a while, he could deceive some fool into believing he was a distinguished German national, and it was on those rare occasions either I or one of his other friends would introduce him as Heinrich Schliemann, who discovered what he thought were the ruins of ancient Troy. Jim would invariably look his victim in the eye, put a hand gently on their shoulder and, still using that terrible accent, say: "Please, call me Heinrich."

After he left Columbia, I saw Kelly only once in what has become a relatively long life. I went to Europe the spring after Greg was killed and, returning to the States, went on to California to remove the chill of a cold French season from my bones. I returned from Europe aboard the old Queen Elizabeth, not the Q.E. Two, Three or Four, and took a bus to St. Louis, where I arranged to drive what some, surely with a smile, used to call a "new used car" to Los Angeles for a dealer who paid for the gas, oil and modest food expenses. In other words, more cheeseburgers. In those days, the large automotive assembly plants were mainly in the Midwest and there was some profit in hiring dopes like me to drive late model cars to the West Coast where other dopes would buy them for inflated prices. Under the arrangement, I was given five days to get from St. Louis to Los Angeles, an ample allowance unless one elected to stop, only 125 miles into a 2,000 mile trip, in Columbia to visit with friends for two or three days. That's exactly what I did, which meant I had to drive straight through once I renewed the trip or forfeit my fuel and food allowance.

By the grace of the patron saint of dopes or some other divine source, I barely made it to California in time to deliver the car and get reimbursed for the money, my only money, that I'd spent on gas and food. With that cash, I found a truly cheap hotel where I slept for a continuous 14 hours to compensate for the almost continuous drive from Missouri to California. Once restored, I left Los Angeles, propelled by my right thumb as I hitch-hiked up the coast highway to Oakland, all my gear packed in a small, blue canvas bag. The details of the trip - like so many of the details in this narrative - have, lucky for you, either been dimmed by or completely lost in time. But I do remember an all-night diner where one of my rides deposited me after dark on the day I left L.A. The place was empty except for the short-order cook, who turned out to be a displaced Missourian from Booneville, a town just down the road from Columbia. I was tempted to think "small world," but resisted the temptation when I realized my thoughts were already banal enough. The only other recollection of that day-long trip was the ride across the Bay Bridge to Oakland which I made on some kind of public transportation.

The week I spent with Kelly in Oakland would have been uneventful had he not attempted to dent his own skull on the concrete floor of a beer hall. We were, of course, drinking beer and Jim leaned back in his chair to the point where the front legs were imprudently far from the ground. He fell backward and there were two ominously loud sounds, which I later realized were made by his beer bottle bursting into miniscule shards and the back of Kelly's head striking an incredibly hard surface. He lay there on his back, stunned momentarily, and then muttered the mandatory "son-of-a-bitch" as the management and some of the customers rushed over to determine whether he was dead or alive. Someone with authority, most likely the bar owner or manager, called an ambulance under the possible assumption that a body lying around on the floor was bad for business. The next I knew we were barreling through the streets of Oakland in the back of a glistening white ambulance with the siren going full blast and cars scattering from our path. Jim lay on his back, bitching about the needlessness of hospital treatment and telling me, over and over, he'd rather have a beer. I might have responded "yeah, yeah" had I not been thinking: "This beats the hell out of hitch-hiking."

Kelly sustained a good thump on his hard head, but was otherwise no worse for the experience. I knew he was his old self when one of the hospital attendants asked him his name and he replied: "Please, call me Heinrich."

I left Oakland several days later to return home, and that was the last we saw of each other. We simply lost touch, as friends often do when their geographic objectives fail to coincide. But I remember Jim with fondness and will always associate him with one terrific ambulance ride.

QUINCE

Laura must have known that Acapulco in early August would be a stifling hellhole, but she convinced Marie, Jack and me that a weekend spent bathing in its calm, as yet unpolluted Pacific waters, and lounging on its fine beaches would provide a refreshing change from Taxco's crisp mountain air. As a result, we bought the package and took off in my car one Friday down the old highway that wound its way tortuously and literally to the water. Acapulco is only a paltry seven feet above sea level.

The old road had been put through in 1927, finally connecting the town to the great northern population centers, particularly Mexico City, and paving the way for a resurgence in the area's fortunes. A newer highway was destined for completion in 1955, but we were five years too early for that improvement and had to endure a slow, kidney-jolting drive over miles of crummy road. It was one switch back after another and my foot rode the brake to the point where I almost forgot how to accelerate.

At the time, Acapulco was Mexico's most popular seaside resort, but it had not quite attained the international reputation for glitz it would assume in the 1960s and 70s when it became a Latin Miami Beach just as the Miami area was developing a Spanish character of its own from the Cuban immigrants who had fled the Castro revolution. It was before a thing called FONATUR, which is a Mexican government agency responsible for vast projects designed to attract tourist revenues, took pristine beaches and turned them into Cancun and Ixtapa, which is to say they out-Miami Beached Miami Beach and out-glitzed Acapulco where social and environmental problems would eventually surface that derived, I've heard, from poorly controlled development that was at once its success and failure. And it was before the John Huston film based on the Tennessee Williams play, "Night of the Iguana," was shot at Puerto Vallarta, up the coast from Acapulco, and made that obscure little community an international tourist destination.

Unlike the soon to be built resorts at Cancun and Ixtapa and, momentarily, setting aside the spectacular pre-Columbian ruins in the region, Acapulco had a substantial recorded history. The place had been used by the Spanish for shipbuilding purposes as early as the 1530s. Its main attraction, originally, was a fine harbor, which in the early days would become an important base for trade with the Orient. The community would later lapse into obscurity and remain little more than a fishing village until the 1927 road was put through and its water and beaches were made accessible to the rest of the country.

We caught Acapulco at a fortunate time in its resort history. The major hotels on the cliffs high above the reasonably unspoiled beaches were splendidly maintained, and the warm Pacific waters offshore were still clean. There was poverty, but not on the scale that would develop a few years later along with the petty crime that would with other problems tarnish the city's reputation. Even at that time, though, an armed guard was posted overnight outside the motel where we found accommodations. The young man, probably of Indian descent, wore fatigues and carried a vintage military rifle. As he made his nightly rounds, the sound of his footfalls blended with the sound of water lapping on the afternoon beach across the boulevard.

Laura and I spent the two mornings of that weekend at Playa Caleta when it was still fashionable to use the morning beach. We weren't trying to be fashionable, only to enjoy the cooler part of the day in a setting away from our friends, who preferred to putter around town looking for God-knows-what. We met them both days after lunch at the afternoon beach where we had drinks at the only cabana on that broad stretch of sand. Marie, never one to keep opinions to herself, had an intense aversion to the Acapulco summer climate "Jesus, it's hot," became her anthem, and I could tell that Laura, after a while, had tired of the comment. She thrived on heat and humidity but, more fundamentally, she'd been brought up by parents who kept their minor complaints to themselves. By the end of the weekend, Laura and Marie were barely speaking to each other and Jack, who rarely spoke under the most conversational of circumstances, was virtually mute. I, meanwhile, was forced to speak for the group as we made the rounds of the cliff-top hotels, where we had cocktails in the evenings and watched a variety of entertainments that didn't seem to entertain my companions. I ordered drinks, and offered an occasional comment to ward off a general silence that threatened to cripple if not destroy our brief holiday. On several occasions, the mood seemed to brighten, sometimes the result of a friendlier remark from Laura or something unexpected from Jack. Once, for no apparent reason, he broke the silence with a few lines from an old song I vaguely recognized. His voice, low and not especially tuneful, was a welcome break as he sang:

He was the best president we ever had

But we shot him

We shot him dead.

I assumed the lyric referred to Jack's take on Mexican political life and was a device that polished off one of his private thoughts, but I also understood the truth was probably a good deal more bizarre. These fleeting moments of socialization were usually vetoed by Marie with yet another "Jesus, it's hot," which she now knew was the surest way to annoy Laura.

The heat and humidity remained constant that weekend, which assured that Marie would neither relent nor repent her incessant obnoxiousness. It also assured a return drive to Taxco that was only a little less difficult than Cortes' retreat from Tenochtitlan with a thoroughly pissed off swarm of Aztecs on his Spanish ass. The mood, had it been sullen, would have been an improvement, and the drive seemed to take forever. The only bright spot I could determine was the cooling temperatures, which would not justify another "Jesus, it's hot" from Marie.

Jack, whose long-term romance with Marie had died of inertia several years before I met them, was a close friend of Marie's husband, Richard, who not only knew about the relationship but encouraged it. The affair, I gathered from things Mary Beth told me, freed him from the neurotic distractions Marie had brought years earlier to their self-imposed shotgun marriage. He married her out of a sense of responsibility or guilt or for the hell of it when she told him she was pregnant with his child. She actually believed it, mainly because she'd missed a couple of periods, and they tied the old knot before the flow resumed and they knew otherwise. Rather than untie it, partially to annoy disapproving parents on both sides, they elected to remain together and go their separate ways, eventually making the marriage serve as a kind of holding company for their joint assets. And as those assets accumulated, the maintenance of their union seemed all the more reasonable.

Richard, who speculated in real estate and murkier things with old money he'd gotten from his family, had served with Jack in something they called "the mountain troops" during the war. Outwardly, they were quite different, I was told, but they shared a number of central characteristics that drew them into a strong friendship. They were about the same age, which made them older than most of the army men they served with, and both were introspective to the point where their long silences were often taken by others for rudeness. And sometimes it was. But they seemed to understand each other without verbal explanations, perhaps because their mildly eccentric personalities were generated by some mysterious yet similar force.

When the war ended, Jack settled in New York, attracted by a teaching position, and reestablished contact with Richard, who introduced him to Marie. They, Jack and Marie, initially "came together with a clang," Marie told Mary Beth, but the juice slowly seeped out of the relationship and they were finally left with a solid friendship that both valued more than the old physical union. They had learned, as I would one day learn, that friendships are more enduring than romance because they are easier to sustain.

Marie, who affected city roots, had actually grown up somewhere in the wilds of New York's Westchester County, and been shipped away at an appropriate age to attend one of those New England women's colleges - either Radcliffe, Smith or Wellesley - that were so detached from my mid-western, land-grant public school consciousness. She eventually escaped to The City, where she studied art, screwed Richard into a strange marriage, and established herself as a formidable teacher and competent painter who knew her way around the established art world. She had not come to Taxco to learn anything about painting, although she may well have thought the change of scene might tell her something she needed to know about herself. No such luck.

Oddly, the rancor between Laura and Marie was gone the day after our return from Acapulco. There was no formal reconciliation between them, only a resumption of their normal friendliness as though nothing had happened. I didn't pretend to understand it and, most likely at the time, made some kind of chauvinistic assumption that attributed the behavior to their gender. Men, I would have figured, were consistent enough to maintain a grudge.

DIECISEIS

The small group at the Humboldt grew socially closer as the season wore on and we developed the habit of gathering for drinks every evening, usually in Tony's bar, before we went our separate ways or returned for one of Trixie's Teutonic dinners. Tony - whose glistening black hair, combed straight back, and incessantly white teeth below a carefully groomed mustache that made him look like a parody of some silent screen matinee idol - usually joined us for an early drink before the demands of his business took him elsewhere. I think he enjoyed the ritual and the opportunity to dispense local gossip or some recollection from what we soon discovered was a colorful past. He was one of those people who had a knack for stumbling into unusual situations, none of them historically or in any other way significant, but strange or interesting for smaller reasons. On a recent trip to Mexico City, Tony told us one evening, he had gotten into a small hotel service elevator to avoid the crowded main lifts that serviced the lobby area. It was the elevator that was small, not the hotel, as he discovered when it stopped at the next floor down and three men crowded into the cage with him. The door closed behind them and they were half way to the main floor before he realized one of the three was a corpse supported upright on each side by the other two men. I would have suspected something sinister, murder at the very least, and been very uncomfortable in that miniature elevator, but Tony was merely curious. His curiosity was satisfied at the landing when the door opened and the corpse and its handlers were met by an orderly of some kind with a stretcher. The corpse, it turned out, had suffered a fatal coronary or something equally terminal in his hotel room, and someone decided to use the under-sized service elevator rather than the main ones out of deference to the surviving guests. The deceased man's chin, Tony recalled, was slumped on his chest and his eyes were closed. But his eyebrows seemed arched and his forehead furrowed as if, Tony said, death had come as a complete surprise to him. That's probably the way most of us look, Jack observed, before the undertakers straighten our eyebrows and iron out the furrows.

Early one morning after Tony had closed his bar and the others had gone in various directions for the evening, I returned with Laura to the Humboldt and we retired to our separate rooms. We were both worn out from a long day and night, and I was soon immersed in the kind of sleep known only to those who drink too much. It's a state somewhere between life and death, maybe a bit closer to the latter.

Only moments later, it seemed, the considerable depth of my slumber wasn't enough to insulate me from the battering on my door and the pitiful wailing that came from the other side. Had I been Irish and superstitious, I would have thought all the banshees in the world had come to roost on my threshold. As it was, I stumbled out of bed, naked, and managed to pull on a pair of pants as I staggered (and that's exactly the right word) through the darkness to a door that continued to act as an instrument for someone who desperately wanted to be heard. That someone, I soon learned, was Marie Pritchard, whose trembling figure stood before me once I'd fumbled the door to an open position. "God damn," she said, pointing behind her. "God damn son-of-a-bitch." I looked down the hall and saw nothing, but she continued to point and finally provided me with a broader clue. "Those bastards," she said. "Those miserable bastards." In a less foggy state, I would have now known there was more than one of them.

Only half conscious, I managed to partially grasp the situation. Barefooted and shirtless, I ran down the hall and the stairs beyond to find two Mexican teenagers, who fled the open doorway when they saw this half-naked fool running full tilt at them. They were half way to their ultimate destination by the time I sailed through the doorway onto the cobblestone street, which was wet with recent rainfall. I made a 90 degree turn and sprinted after the boys whose white shirts were still visible but fading in the distance. Despite my bare feet, slapping against the wet cobblestones, I managed to pick up speed, although the odds against my overtaking them were somewhere between big and astronomical. Those odds were soon rendered moot, mainly because the cool night air began to revive me and I abruptly realized the futility of the contest. It not only became clear I couldn't catch them, it was even clearer it would be plain folly to try. What would I have done had I succeeded?

I literally skidded to a stop and stood motionless for a few moments in the silent street to collect my jumbled thoughts. The air was chilly and I had no idea what this business with crazy Marie was about. As I learned, it wasn't about much. She had neither been raped nor seriously robbed, although she may have been the victim of the pettiest larceny in the annals of crime. Marie had left Tony's bar with Jack and gone to a restaurant where they ate and got into a quarrel. The Mexican boys, who sometimes picked up a little loose change helping or hustling tourists, met Marie as she left the restaurant alone in a snit, and offered to see her safely home. Mistaking their youth for innocence, she accepted the offer, not understanding they expected pay for this service. At the Humboldt door, she gave one of them her pocket flashlight to hold as she searched her handbag for the key. The young man, once he learned there would be no pay, refused to return the flashlight, which sent Marie screaming to my door and dispatched me, practically naked, onto a damp cobblestone street. The harmless futility of the whole incident - much like long parts of life itself - makes me think there should be some lesson to be learned from this and other equally unimportant events, but I'm damned if I know what it is.

DIECISIETE

I never knew Tony's last name, but I learned more about him that summer from a series of casual conversations than I knew about some of my close friends and most of my relatives. Strangers sometimes invest us with deep confidences they wouldn't disclose to their spouses or analysts. This seeming anomaly is, however, not so anomalous.

On the other hand, I not only learned but remember his girlfriend Betty's family name, Tomkinson, although her personal history - beyond English origins and the assumption she was in her late 20s or a little older that summer - is pretty much of a mystery to me. I may have neglected her genealogy in favor of her cerulean eyes, tinkling voice and long, slender legs. Or, more probably, I might have asked Betty about herself had I not realized that Tony was very proprietary where she was concerned, and there was no point in giving him the wrong impression. Or, perhaps, the right one. As it was, Betty and I retained a discrete relationship, and I made a few general assumptions about her gauzy history.

She was a Londoner, I knew from casual references she'd made, and she must have been at the end of her teens when the German aerial bombardment or blitz descended on the city in the summer of 1940. She was not a working class girl, which was apparent from her accent, and she probably spent the war in some respectable patriotic uniform, doing respectably patriotic service and waiting for the first respectable opportunity to escape that murderous madness that began with what came to be called "The Battle of Britain."

That battle raged in the skies over southern England from early June to the end of October, with the German air fleet of some 1,400 bombers and 1,000 fighter aircraft pitted against the Royal Air Force and its 700 fighters. In the end, the Germans lost the battle, along with more than 1,700 planes and the chance to invade England. The English lost 915 fighters and, far more regrettably from my point of view, 449 pilots who manned their Hurricane and Spitfire aircraft. Out of frustration, perhaps, the Germans turned to the systematic night bombing of the larger cities, especially London, and that did little more than kill a lot of perfectly innocent people, destroy a good deal of real estate, some of it quite historic, and justify the later allied bombing of German cities, which killed even more innocent people and destroyed even more real estate, some of it just as historic as the English structures.

As almost everyone knows, the Germans eventually lost the war, a fate, in my opinion, they richly deserved. I'm convinced that anyone who'd bomb someone as pretty as Betty deserves what they get.

Tony, when I knew him, was about 35, give or take a year or two. He was the only son of a prosperous Mexico City businessman, who had indulged him most of his life. He'd loaned Tony the money to buy the bar in Taxco, and in the mid-1930s he financed an extended European trip meant to educate, sophisticate and otherwise expand his son's intellectual and social horizons. His father wouldn't have put it that way, Tony told me, but that's what he had in mind. What he didn't have in mind was the Spanish Civil War, which broke out in 1936 and at the time seemed to Tony like an adventure too good to miss while he was in the neighborhood.

Actually, he was in France at the time and had made friends with several French students whose sympathies lay with the Spanish republicans. They went off to war to prove they were serious and Tony tagged along for the hell of it, unable to know the conflict would eventually claim 500,000 to 1,000,000 lives, depending on whose estimates you believe.

The war in Spain - which was a precursor of the Second World War in terms of opposing ideologies and the use of new weapons and tactics - began in Morocco when the Spanish army commanders revolted in resentment against the growing socialist and anti-church direction of the republican government in Madrid. For some perverse reason, all the big wars seem to begin in small, remote places. Show me a god-forsaken backwater country or region, and I'll show you a breeding ground for conflict, particularly if there's an army nearby.

The Spanish insurgents or nationalists were backed by German air power and Italian manpower, supplied by Hitler and Mussolini, while the Russians provided advisors and technicians to the republicans, who were also supported by International brigades composed mainly of communist and left-wing sympathizers from many countries. Tony - who by the time I knew him was more conservative than the insurgents - wound up in one of those brigades and saw enough action to learn that other people's political differences were none of his business.

The insurgents were originally led by several generals but Francisco Franco rose to command and stayed in power, ultimately as head of state, for the rest of his long life. In the war, he gained early control of half the country before the republicans rallied and defeated a large Italian army at Guadalajara in what for the Italians was a rehearsal for future defeats in the bigger war to come. The Italians, I've concluded, made military defeat a virtue, proving in two world wars that - unlike the British, Germans and, originally, the French - you could substantially reduce casualties by simply bungling the job. The French belatedly learned the Italian lesson when they surrendered to the Germans in 1940, avoiding the trench warfare that had decimated a generation of young European men in the First World War. It's not that the Italians are any less courageous or intelligent than the British, French or Germans, it's just that their longer history of modern, as opposed to tribal, warfare has led them to more civilized notions about those activities. Had Mussolini noted this characteristic in his countrymen, his corpse might not have wound up hanging ignominiously in Milan's Piazzale Loreto.

By 1938, the Germans and Italians had put more resources into the Spanish effort and enabled the nationalists to resume an offensive throughout the country. Rival factions struggling for power within the republican government and the withdrawal of Russian support eventually led to the collapse of republican military forces. A number of major Spanish cities fell to Franco as the resistance melted away. The republicans surrendered unconditionally in late March.

Tony managed to reach France from Spain and subsequently returned to Mexico, where he lived peacefully and gratefully, he said, throughout the Second World War, alternately attending university classes and working for his father in a number of jobs that convinced both of them he was supremely unsuited for conventional work. His dad, probably disappointed that his son wasn't destined to follow in his mercantile footprints but, like Tony, grateful the boy hadn't been killed in some obscure Spanish field, eventually shelled out money for the bar. And to their mutual surprise, Tony found a business that perfectly suited his amiable temperament and social disposition. He turned out to be his father's son after all, as well as a perfect host and considerable manager who quickly mastered everything from bartending to bookkeeping, learning early on that businesses are sustained by profits. It's a simple concept, he told me, but one that's hard to learn when you're living off a father's generosity. It isn't as hard, I told him, as having poor parents. I doubt he got my point, so I decided to admire him for his success in the face of miniscule odds.

EIGHTEEN

In the late 1940s and early 1950s, there was a lot of work for good jazz musicians in and around St. Louis, especially on Friday and Saturday nights when the bars that employed them were jammed, mostly with people in their 20s. Either with a lone friend or sometimes in dense packs, we'd travel the region seeking out the music and the single young women who, we hoped, were looking for us. The cigarette smoke in most of those places was so thick by mid-evening you couldn't see anything, let alone a prospect, and the noise - composed of music, loud conversation and clattering glassware, among other things - precluded the possibility of any communication other than guttural sounds and simple hand signals. You could point to a beer, hold up a couple of fingers and the bartender or waitress would know you wanted two of those, but it would have been useless to order, say, a very dry straight up Tangueray Gibson, even if you knew what it was. There are those bars in cities around the world where people sit quietly and respectfully listen to musicians, applauding with polite enthusiasm at appropriate intervals. I remember a small club in Paris off the Boulevard Saint Germain, near the Church of Saint Germain Des Pres, where the audience snapped their fingers to demonstrate appreciation, an affectation, I thought, that carried restraint too far. I don't remember much applause in those St. Louis bars, but the musicians seemed to know they were appreciated because the ones that weren't played, though not for long, mainly to empty rooms.

There were regular bars and bars with entertainment throughout the city and the sprawling county with its dozens of municipalities that pinned St. Louis, Missouri against the west bank of the Mississippi River. There were still more bars, some of them in road and whorehouses, across the river in grimy, worn-out, wide-open East St. Louis, Illinois where we sometimes went after closing time in our home community. In an area called The Valley - which was on a bleak, run-down strip of highway outside East St. Louis - there was a rather large selection of unprepossessing whorehouses, all with surprisingly similar but splendidly utilitarian formats. They had bars up front with miniscule dance floors and large juke boxes. Down back hallways were small, cell-like rooms, one after the other, with curtained doorways that provided less privacy than I need to conduct that kind of business. And anyone who wanted to use the lavatories had to walk those halls and listen to the grunts, groans and assorted other sounds that came from the occupied rooms. The unoccupied women usually sat at the bars or one of the tables up front, talking to prospective customers or, perhaps, filing or painting their fingernails.

We sometimes stopped in one of those places for beers and conversation, unable for financial reasons and unwilling for public health concerns to use its principal service. Early one morning, Greg Upp and I arrived for nightcaps which, we calculated, would leave us with exact bridge toll and no more for the return drive to St. Louis. We'd blown most of our money at an uptown club listening to the guitarist Les Paul and his wife, the singer Mary Ford. As we sat at the roadhouse bar and drank, one of the whores - a plain young woman in a flowered cotton smock -approached Greg with the usual proposal. Curious, he asked her the price, which that day was three dollars. "Jesus Christ, lady," he said in a feeble attempt at mock indignation, "that's bloody highway robbery." She looked at him as if he was the world's biggest dope. "Have you been up town lately?" she asked, not waiting for an answer. "I have and I bought a pair of shoes. Do you know what they cost?" About this time we both realized it was the old inflation gambit, and Greg conceded the argument. "You've sold me," he said, "but I'm broke and that's the plain truth." He was pulling his pants pockets inside out to prove the point and, he told me later, was about to ask if she had a credit plan as the woman left in search of a more promising prospect.

Those nights on the "east side" in places with names like Court's Cafe and Chum's all ran together after a while, forming recollections as murky as the industrially-polluted air that made all outdoors over there look like it had been seen through a screen door. And while the air in St. Louis was cleaner since the introduction of hard coal for general heating purposes, the bars after a while took on the same kind of similarity. We probably traveled hundreds of miles a year, possibly thousands, mostly on Fridays and Saturdays when we were in town, scouting the bars that had gained new currency or attending the familiar old ones. But our home base was a strip of Del mar Boulevard, not more than a couple of miles long, in the west end of St. Louis, where we usually met at the

Mainline or Barrel bars or at the Windemere, Dick's Liquor Store (which wasn't a store) or Beffa's. The only one that didn't have entertainment was Beffa's, if you excluded its bartenders, Reno and Gino, who had their entertaining moments. Reno, on slow nights, would mix Pusse Cafes, a drink constructed of various liquors layered by weight and color into a small vessel until he wound up with a nicely stripped beverage that tasted something like sludge. A small group of us would cluster around the bar, watching intently as he carefully poured layer after tricky layer and probably thinking to ourselves it was time to get a life.

The Mainline usually had a band at night, which attracted the conventional young crowd. There was also an early evening group of regulars made up of a half dozen middle-aged men who daily stopped for drinks, usually beer, with the regularity of Greenwich Mean Time. One of them, Earl, an automobile mechanic for a nearby dealership, told me one evening he'd once been a newspaper reporter for a major Los Angeles daily. He lost his job and was nationally black-balled, he said, because he knew about a murder the powerful publisher, William Randolph Hearst, had committed in a rage against a man who had come on to Marian Davies, Hearst's long-tenured mistress. The deed had been done, Earl revealed, aboard Hearst's yacht off the California coast and the body had been unceremoniously dumped overboard. I listened to the story only because I liked Earl and he'd bought me a beer. I didn't believe it then and I don't believe it now, and I attribute the details in his story to rumors he'd heard in the 1920s when Hearst and Davies were the objects, with other celebrities, of popular speculation. The story, though, has remained with me all these years and I remember the quiet, off-hand manner with which Earl told it as he sat on a barstool in his white coveralls. He was either one hell of a story-teller or he'd come to believe it himself, perhaps as a device to loan interest to an otherwise ordinary life. If that was his motive, he succeeded in more ways than one by creating, for me, still another mystery. I've always wondered how Earl managed to work all day as a mechanic and appear, on his way home from the garage, in a pair of immaculately clean coveralls. There was more to Earl, William Randolph Hearst aside, than met the eye.

Some of the other regulars, Earl's friends, knew I was a sometime student, usually low on cash and other negotiable resources, and they would often buy me beers out of a sense of generosity that was partly character-driven and partly the result of their own drinking. Alcohol breeds a lot of things, including generosity. The owner of the Mainline, Sam, once heard me refuse one of those offers on the grounds my current bottle was not yet empty. He got me aside a few minutes later and looked intently in my direction to telegraph the gravity of the coming message. "Never," he instructed, "refuse a free drink." He said he'd credit me and I could drink the freebies at my leisure, either the same night, the next week or the next month, whatever. Following his instructions, I soon accumulated a backlog amounting to several dozen bottles, which only proved that I was a pretty slow drinker. But Sam seemed satisfied with the arrangement and this personal beer inventory gave me a sense of security I'd not known since the day I took my first drink.

My bar room friends, including Greg and Jerry, were mainly people I knew from high school. Most of them, like Jerry and I, had gone into some branch of military service after graduation. And most of them had, on discharge, returned to schools, some to Washington or St. Louis Universities in the city or, again like us, to the state university at Columbia. Still others went further afield, a few to institutions in the far west or the east but most of the remainder to small universities and colleges throughout the mid-west. With a few exceptions, we were in school about the same time, which brought us together in St. Louis for various holidays, vacations or individual reasons. I don't mean that this fairly large and diverse group of individuals met at planned intervals or that we were all close friends. Not in the least. We had, mainly, the high school and a few shared experiences in common. Those commonalities, when combined with drink, were sufficient to create a reunion effect when one or another of us would meet in some out-of-the-way bar in an obscure corner of the county or over in Illinois. The sight of a familiar face when you're half gassed in a room full of strangers has a reassuring effect, something similar to a return to the family farm after a long and hard absence. And like the return to the farm, these meetings sometimes revealed why you left home in the first place. Some of these old acquaintances, you rediscovered, were people you really didn't like that much in high school.

One night over the Christmas holidays in 1949, Greg and I were in The Barrel, drinking with a few chums from the old high school, when we met two young women. Greg was uncharacteristically restrained that evening, which only means he didn't insult one or both of them before we had a chance to get acquainted. He was, strangely, a model of good behavior, almost charming, in fact, and this deviant rectitude on his part enabled us to join them at their table for a few drinks and a good deal of conversation that eventually got us an invitation to their nearby apartment. As we left the bar and went out into the cold December air, I could scarcely believe that any man in Greg's company could get this lucky. Greg was a good person to drink with, but he was the kiss of death in the romance department. He was more likely to get you arrested than screwed.

We left my car parked near The Barrel and walked the three blocks to their apartment, where we settled in their living room, briefly, before Greg showed his true colors. "Do you have a shower?" he asked one of the women in the middle of a conversation that had nothing to do with personal hygiene. She acknowledged that they did, barely noting the question and, possibly, thinking he simply wanted to pee. As he excused himself and headed for the bathroom, I knew better and wasn't surprised a few minutes later when we heard, down the short hallway, the sound of shower water beating insistently against their porcelain tub. "What's that noise?" one of them ask, knowing the answer but not quite willing to believe it.

"He's taking a shower," I admitted, knowing now there would be nothing miraculous this Christmas season.

NINETEEN

Jerry and I met at the St. Louis high school we both attended and where we both met Greg. The institution was mainly distinguished, as far as I could tell, on two particular counts. It was the smallest public high school in the city and the only one without a football team. The irony in that second count was the expanse of ground, once employed for football, that was spread out in front of the building, The sport had been abolished from our school some years earlier when a student athlete had died as the result of a game-inflicted injury. Or, at least, that was the story. It would have made more sense had our school been a private one rather than part of a large, urban educational system where football was relentlessly played everywhere else. It wasn't fair to our student body, but it was a good lesson in life.

Jerry and I were either 15 or 16 when we first came to know each other, and when he lived with his parents in a small, eccentric, two-storied house on a triangular corner lot. The house's eccentricities were both internal and external, climaxed, for me, by a triangular ash pit, which in those days held the residues from coal furnaces, that fit neatly into the triangle formed at the very rear of the miniscule back yard. Inside, the scale also seemed small, almost as though the place had been built for dwarfs, although each of the three family members were above average height. Jerry played, or more accurately, struggled with the clarinet and his infrequent practice usually made his Chow dog, Chang Fu Tang Sun IV. howl in anguished protest when he managed to get the instrument to produce something in high register. It sometimes made me howl in protest, no matter the register.

Jerry's parents, Charlie and Jeanette, had divorced when he was very young, and remarried when he was 12. He told me he had also been circumcised that same year, but I don't think there was any special connection between the two events other than the fact they were both painful, one in the short term and the other over time, and served no useful purpose. Jeanette - whose maiden name, Tracy, was given to Jerry as a middle name - held an office job of some kind, and Charlie was an automobile mechanic who hated Communists. Without trying to be clever, he called them "Commonists," and blamed them for every negative thing from bad government to foul weather. And he did it before it became generally popular.

Charlie and Jeanette were destined to divorce a second time after Jerry left home and, this time, I think there was some relationship between the two events. Implicit in their separation was the recognition that the kid was gone and there was no longer any need to keep up the pretense. Jerry seemed to accept their final rupture with a certain sense of inevitability and, perhaps, wonder at their ability to have remained together for as long as they did in a marriage marked principally, he once said, for its "rampant incompatibility."

By any standard, Jerry was a reasonably bright guy who eventually achieved a university degree and some success in a dogged corporate job, but he had a few rough edges. The common courtesies often eluded him and the word "fuck" was an entrenched part of his spoken vocabulary. His wife mentioned those tendencies in him many years later after his death, but said he was amazingly "smooth" considering his background. By that, she meant Charlie and Jeanette were something less than model parents. I'm sure she knows more about them than I do.

Still married when we finished high school and enlisted in the Marine Corps with several other friends, Jerry's parents moved across the state to Kansas City only weeks before we left for boot camp at Parris Island, South Carolina. Jerry made the move with them, but returned to St. Louis several days before our scheduled departure to participate in the round of parties that often attended military enlistments, marriages and other seminal events in the lives of young people. For those few days, he stayed with my mother and me in the small apartment we'd occupied since my early childhood when the economic depression of the 1930s and my father's boozing conspired to evict us from more prosperous circumstances down south.

The night before we left for boot camp there was a big party, a party so big we, meaning the young men, all wore our only suits and took dates, who wore their best dresses. I took Jean, who was what we use to call a "steady" girl friend to indicate absolute exclusivity in the relationship. I don't think Jerry took anyone, perhaps the result of his transient circumstances, which may have led him to drink more than he usually did and enough to make him pass out and throw up over the front of his suit and the back seat of a friend's family car. Luckily, I missed the big heave because Jean and I left the party early to say our personal goodbyes, which involved a good deal of deep kissing and the rubbing together of bodies in an apartment entryway. It was still a few years before puberty and consummation became synonymous terms.

I was home asleep, sound asleep, when several friends delivered Jerry's unconscious body to my mother's doorstep, apologizing for his condition but not providing much of an explanation before they fled into the night. That was left for me the next morning, shortly after I'd gone into our only bathroom and discovered the wreck of Jerry's suit in the tub. That garment, once a crisp glen plaid, had been rendered a sorry jumble of twisted cloth and dried effluence. And it had taken on an unpleasant odor that wasn't there when the cloth left the mill. My mother, decent middle-class woman that she was, expressed concern about Jerry's condition as well as his behavior, which I ingeniously attributed to a "Mickey Finn." Everyone in those days, including my abstemious mother, knew that a "Mickey" was a cocktail some villain had laced with knock-out drops to entrap an innocent victim. I portrayed Jerry as the innocent victim, a blatant lie my mother bought like Seward bought Alaska. She not only bought it, she got Jerry out of bed to make certain he had a good breakfast before she went off to work. She practically dragged his beat-up carcass, wearing a too-short pair of my old jeans, to the breakfast table and force fed him bacon and a couple of eggs, despite his pitiful protests and repeated assertions that a cup of black coffee would be quite sufficient, thank you very much, and, under his breath, god damn it. The experience apparently made a considerable impression on Jerry. For years afterward, all you had to do was make some vague reference to my mother and he'd say: "Eat that goddamn egg."

Jerry married a young woman, a graduate student he met at the university, and they eventually settled in one of the middle-sized cities on the Great Plains where he rose to a management job with one of the utilities. He and his wife, Ruth, had two sons, which they named Mark and Matthew. If they'd had two others, he told me later in life, they'd have named them Luke and John because he didn't like "that Randy, Sandy bullshit." Despite the biblical quality of those names, Jerry had neither inclination nor much sympathy for formal religious practice. He was a charter member of the Greg Upp Religious Exclusion Society, as far as I knew. Knowing this, I was surprised to learn that he and his wife had not only joined but become very active in a local Unitarian church. Jerry explained during one of our infrequent meetings that he and Ruth decided their young sons needed moral instruction, if only to enable them to make independent decisions later in life about their eternal beliefs. But he also said his church was a pretty flexible institution, which once assigned him to interview a prospective minister. He conducted that interview at the old Playboy Club in Chicago, where he learned, among other things, that the young prospect could play the guitar and sing. One of his favorite songs was:

> I don't care
> if it rains or freezes
> As long as I've got
> my plastic Jesus
> Riding on the
> dashboard of my car...

The man didn't get the job, but he and Jerry drank the night away in a succession of Rush Street saloons, which is what Jerry told me he had in mind in the first place. "We got along just fine," Jerry said, "but it was clear he wouldn't go over with the more conservative members of the congregation." I couldn't imagine who these people were, particularly when Jerry, describing that evening in Chicago, said the only place he'd done more drinking than on Rush Street was in the basement of his church. The irony was profound, he said, because a local ordinance banned the sale of alcohol within a specified distance from any "place of worship" in the city.

Jerry had an enormous capacity for drink and I got the impression his early retirement from the utility wasn't entirely voluntary. I judged his affinity for a couple of martinis or more at lunch may have been a contributing factor. Drinking, too, may have shortened his life, although he'd gone on the wagon several years before a massive coronary malfunction of some kind put him away for good. I suspect he wasn't entirely surprised, a suspicion based on our last phone conversation a month or so before the end. He seemed uncharacteristically wistful, telling me we'd known each other a long time in a way that suggested the time had nearly run out. In his case, it nearly had.

Shortly after Jerry's death, Ruth found a file in his home office labeled "Smut," which she promptly threw, unopened, into the trash. Later that day, she told a woman friend about the file, and the friend was amazed her curiosity hadn't been stronger. Ruth began to think about the file and it wasn't long before she went to the garage where several dozen plastic trash bags had been temporarily stored pending the pick-up day. It took more than an hour to find the file, crumpled but intact, and only a few moments to discover its contents. Jerry had saved two "girlie" magazines he and Ruth had purchased out of curiosity on some long-forgotten trip. The magazines were completely innocuous, especially by later standards, but the label, "Smut," said something about the droll person who'd devised it.

VEINTE

Frank Mirabella had been in Mexico City for less than six months in the late summer of 1940 when the exiled Russian revolutionary leader Leon Trotsky had his head cleaved by a Spanish-born Stalinist agent. Only a few months earlier, Mirabella told me, Trotsky, his wife and grandson had survived a machine gun attack on his heavily guarded house, adding further evidence to the widely held suspicion that there's very little subtlety in Communism.

Until he was outmaneuvered by Stalin, Trotsky was generally regarded as Lenin's successor to head the Soviet Union, that vast collection of races, cultures, time zones, geography and contradictions that would one day collapse under the weight of its own diversity. Trotsky had served the Russian revolution in a variety of important ways, most notably as organizer of the Red Army, a motley collection of workers and peasants who in a desperate civil war defeated the anti-revolutionary forces and their American, British and Japanese allies.

After the war and during Lenin's final illness in the early 1920s, Trotsky's preoccupation with military and external affairs enabled Stalin to gain control of the communist party administration, and gradually assert his authority. By 1925, Trotsky had lost effective power and two years later was expelled from the Party. He was deported from Russia early in 1929, and settled briefly in Turkey, later in France and finally in Mexico where Stalin's long, vindictive arm finally caught up with him. That bloody event - carried out not far from where Mirabella lived at the time - made Frank feel like a witness to history. He had come to Mexico to study the language and culture, but an important motivation had been the lost republican cause in the recent Spanish civil war. The revolutionary spirit was still strong in Mexico in those days, and there had been many Mexican volunteers who went to Spain to fight with the international brigades against the native-grown fascists and their German and Italian supporters. Frank felt a strong kinship with the communists, probably the result of his American working-class background and depression-era upbringing. His immigrant parents had not participated in the prosperity of the 1920s and subsequent events and conditions in the following decade had done little to make him feel the economic system was working to his benefit. Looking elsewhere, Frank had learned a great deal about the Russian revolution and knew more about its central figures, Leon Trotsky included, than most people outside the Soviet Union. He knew Trotsky had been born in the Ukraine in 1879 and was first arrested as a revolutionary at the tender age of 19. As they were prone to do, the authorities sent the young man to Siberia, where he promptly escaped and went to London to join Lenin in 1902. A few years later, he was back in Russia, where he was arrested, sent to Siberia and, once again, escaped. It was getting monotonous but revolutionaries - judging by their incredibly long, dull speeches - are apparently impervious to monotony. Trotsky carried on, working as a revolutionary organizer in central Europe and elsewhere until 1917 when he returned to Russia from America to become chairman of the Petrograd soviet during the October revolution. And the rest, just like that which preceded it, is history.

Frank knew all this stuff and more. He knew all the details of Trotsky's rise in the Soviet ranks and just as much about the man's stunning decline. He knew things about Trotsky that Stalin probably didn't know. He knew, for example, that Trotsky had dimples. He knew it and insisted on proving it to me by digging out an old book with a grainy photograph of the man and his dimples.

He knew that Joseph Stalin's original name was Djugashvili, and that he was born in a village in the Caucasian Mountains of Georgia. Stalin was booted out of a seminary for his revolutionary opinions, and spent the next years either in prison or traveling in that great tradition of those who want to bring down existing governments and institutions. Frank thought it would have been just like any other dull job had Stalin and his Boishevik associates not managed to seize power in Russia.

Stalin not only eliminated Trotsky, but several years earlier got rid of thousands of real or imagined enemies, mainly veteran revolutionaries and army officers, in those sweeping purges that made some of his foreign supporters suspect that perhaps the socialist experiment was not quite what they thought it was. His pact with Hitler a few years later was further confirmation of those suspicions.

Stalin essentially made himself prime minister in 1941 and as Commisar of Defense and Marshall of the Soviet Union directed the war effort against the Germans who invaded his country that year. But he sorely missed those professional soldiers he'd executed a few years earlier and probably, in Frank's opinion, only beat the Germans because of the courage of the Soviet peoples, vastness of the geography and Hitler's enormous military incompetence. And while Frank wasn't willing to credit foreign aid as a factor in the German defeat, I knew the war material supplied by the United States had at the very least been useful in that destructive enterprise.

Stalin died in 1953 and was embalmed and buried in the Kremlin wall with Lenin, where he remained until he fell into disfavor and was removed to a plain grave outside the wall eight years later. Since he had helped to erect and eventually presided over a godless state, the concept of an afterlife was one that Stalin, despite his early religious training, had probably discarded. In that case, his removal from the Kremlin wall probably had little personal effect on him one way or the other.

The death of Leon Trotsky several miles from Frank Mirabella's residence turned out to be the climactic event in both their lives. It was curtains for Trotsky, of course, and it was, in a way, also the end for poor Frank. For him, nothing beyond that assassination seemed important, not because he held Trotsky in any particular esteem but mostly because he saw himself so close to what he considered an important historical event. It was as if he'd witnessed the assassination of Lincoln or Nelson's victory at Trafalgar. He thought of his proximity to Trotsky's death as a supreme stroke of historical good fortune when in reality it was, for him, a personal disaster attributable to his own quirky mentality.

Mirabella somehow remained in Mexico throughout the war, evading U.S. military service through some means that must have been legal because he was, when I knew him, able to cross the border with impunity. These circumstances gave rise to a rumor that he had been an American spy in Mexico, where he could gather all kinds of Latin American and other information, but I have my doubts. Frank just didn't have the stuff. He was reasonably smart, but he couldn't keep his mouth shut and he was totally devoid of personal discipline, let alone courage. If through some really strange set of circumstances he had served as an agent, I'd give odds he botched the job.

Frank eventually lost his enthusiasm for left-wing politics and gradually moved to the right in his views. I think he was persuaded less by Stalin's perfidy than by his own advancing interest in material things. He began to associate with affluent people, which is possible because the wealthy are not always smart. And Frank was just clever enough to recognize the visiting Americans he could fool with his fluent Spanish and superficial knowledge of local history and culture. As he mingled with these people - who provided him with expensive meals and other entertainments, but little in the way of revenue - he developed a taste, if not the means, for those things money can buy. By the time I knew him, he had adopted the manner and some of the preferences of his wealthy associates, and usually managed to disguise his genuinely modest circumstances. He told anyone who'd listen that he worked as a Spanish instructor because he thought everyone should have occupation, and he rarely disclosed his personal address, which I suspect would have instantly revealed his true situation.

Frank had also joined The Church, which he attended with more than ordinary devotion, and regarded his left-leaning youth as an aberration attributable to his early lack of intellectual sophistication. The inference, I gathered, was that he'd gained that quality in subsequent years.

He had no real family other than a few rumored stateside relatives he hadn't seen in years and apparently had no intention of seeing any time soon. And as far as I could see, he had no real friends. To anyone with ordinary good sense, Mirabella was a pompous, self-deluding, semi-cowardly, lying leech and at least several other things that are less than pleasant. Normally, you'd think a person of his circumstances and qualities would be lonely and alienated, a bitter ex-patriot with a nasty, even venomous disposition. Not so. Old Frank seemed more than content, perhaps because he'd come to believe the fabulous bullshit about himself he'd so readily dumped on anyone who gave him the opportunity. Or, maybe he realized his life, for all practical purposes, had ended with the death of Leon Trotsky and all the rest was just gravy.

TWENTY-ONE

At the end of the spring semester in 1950, not long before I left for Mexico, the four of us had dinner together for the last time. It wasn't until years later that Jerry and I began referring to the meeting as The Last Supper, recognizing one critical difference between our meal and the biblical one. Everyone in our group - including Tom, Greg, Jim and yours truly - wanted to be Jesus.

We ate at Ernie's Steak House in Columbia, where we usually had dinner at the first of the month before our resources ran too low for further extravagance. We not only ate together, we invariably ordered the same dinner - broiled pork chops, French fries and garlic-buttered rolls. Not exactly the heart-smart menu, but cholesterol was an unknown word in those days and most realists expected to have some kind of large coronary event in their 60s.

I remember the evening more vividly than most, probably because it was the last time I saw Greg. As we ate, Greg's attention was drawn to a plate of food delivered to an elderly man at a nearby table. The geezer had apparently ordered a cutlet of some kind smothered in the whitest cream gravy ever made, a sauce of sorts that also coated his mashed potatoes and oozed against a large scoop of cottage cheese, also pure white. "Jesus, god" Greg said, nodding in the man's direction as he cut into his pork chop, "he'd better stick a piece of parsley on his plate before he goes snow blind."

We were in particularly good spirits, partially because the semester and its final examinations were over and also because we each had individual expectations. Greg would soon graduate, spend the summer doing Archaeology in the Missouri boondocks and go on to Northwestern University in the fall for graduate work in Anthropology. Jim planned to spend the next month in St. Louis before he went to California, and Jerry - who would remain steadfastly in Columbia until his graduation a year or so later - was to move in with his girl friend and future wife the next week. I, not surprisingly, was looking forward to the Mexican trip. And, with the fatal exception of Greg's attempt to cross the dark road with a six-pack, we managed, each of us, to realize our expectations for the summer.

We were, obviously, unaware of what was about to happen in the Orient, which may explain how the North Koreans managed to pull off a surprise attack on their neighbors to the south. In any event it would have surprised us even if they'd announced their plans with full-page display ads in all the major American newspapers. We weren't paying attention. Greg, who read the papers with some degree of seriousness, focused mainly on issues of social justice and baseball. Jerry read only those books mandate by his coursework, and Jim usually scrutinized the labels on his beer bottles. I read books that interested me, usually ignoring the ones that represented class assignments. We were encapsulated in our own little world and didn't care much about the wider one that invariably governed everything.

There were usually a number of familiar faces at Ernie's, mostly other student military veterans splurging, as we were, early in the month before the weeks of enforced austerity set in. That night, I saw George Chandler across the room at a table with what I guessed was his own date and another couple. George and I knew each other from the St. Louis neighborhood where I lived for a good part of my childhood and from the high school we both attended. We were friendly, if not friends, during the early years, but somewhere in our mid-teens George began to avoid me. He'd gesture or nod as we passed, but he went obviously out of his way to deflect any conversation, especially when he was with others. I gradually noticed the change, but gave it little thought, mostly because our relationship had always been rather distant. The reason for the change in George's behavior toward me remains to this day a matter of speculation, but his motive wasn't all that difficult to understand once I learned that Carl Hammerstein had changed his name to George Chandler.

George, or Carl, was an eight or nine year old boy when he came to the United States in 1936 as part of the rising flood of Jewish refugees from Nazi Germany. With his parents and sister, he settled in an apartment near the one where I lived with my mother. In the next few years, others, like Carl, arrived and the children were quietly integrated into the public schools. At first, they stood quite apart from their American schoolmates, not only the result of thick German accents but also because their conservative European clothing, usually heavy gray wools in the winter and high socks in all but the sultriest weather, were as different from ours as the games we played. Their parents probably retained their thick accents for the rest of their lives, but the children, as children do when left to themselves, rapidly adjusted to the new environment and within a few years spoke and looked like the rest of us. Poor devils. And Carl Hammerstein was no exception.

Carl's family, reduced to modest circumstances in America, had been affluent in Germany. It was that affluence that had enabled them to escape Europe and, perhaps, the death camps where so many Jews were to die a few years later. Although I didn't know it at the time, those conservative gray wools that made the new refugees seem so different were expensive garments, and our cotton corduroy knickers almost certainly looked tacky to those newly impoverished German-Jewish parents.

Carl's father, I'd heard, had been an attorney in Munich, not a good place for a wealthy Jew in the late 1920s and early 30s as Hitler and his Nazis rose to power. And not a good place, I'm sure, for the young son of a wealthy Jew. Carl surely had recollections of the persecution that sent his family packing to America and he must have had his own personal difficulties with former German school friends who were joining the adult onrush to demonize Jews in general and rich ones in particular. Ironically, Carl looked more like the Nordic prototype that Hitler envisioned for the German people than the German people themselves, who are mainly middle-Europeans. While not particularly handsome, Carl was tall and blonde with an athletic build and capacities. At high school, he lettered in swimming and track, developed a mildly arrogant attitude and changed his name to George Chandler. My suspicion, since it originated, has always been that Carl, or George, wanted nothing to do with the past and I was a link to it simply because I knew his real identity, which I always kept to myself. I don't have many virtues, but I can keep a secret when I'm not writing a book. Carl, however, didn't know that.

As we sat in Ernie's, eating and talking about the same old stuff, the sight of George across the room, coupled with something someone said about "Negroes" reminded me of the old neighborhood, which in turn reminded me of O.C. Clark. A big, strong black man of middle years, O.C. was the janitor for a half dozen apartment buildings, including ours, on the block. He was up early on winter mornings to coal the furnaces and dispose of the ashes from the previous night, and he was up early on summer mornings to perform dozens of other chores that extended from simple sweeping to fairly complicated mechanical repairs. He was a jack-of-all-trades, roaming the neighborhood in a continuing effort to keep those aging buildings supplied with heat, operative plumbing and electricity in a depression era when landlords were reluctant to put money into anything.

O.C had an apartment in the basement of one of the buildings under his care, where he lived with his wife and son. I rarely saw his family, who either remained at home or traveled the nearby streetcar line to visit relatives and friends in the black neighborhoods that bordered the downtown area. As a child, I thought of O.C. more as an environmental fixture than as a black man. He was always kind and watchful in respect to me - perhaps because he knew my father wasn't around - and he'd patiently explain what he was doing when I inquired about a task he was on. Once, he gave me a clue to his inner thoughts, but it was only years later that I remembered what he said and meant. White people, he told me when I was about seven or eight, were once black in color. Everyone, he said, was once black. The Caucasian race began with a group of sinners who God strickened with leprosy, turning them white. He didn't say so, but the implication was clearly that the descendents of both groups, good and bad, are easily distinguished to this day by their color. And why not?

The fuel that O.C. shoveled into those apartment building furnaces was bituminous or soft coal, a volatile substance that poured clouds of thick, black smoke into the St. Louis skies. O.C.'s furnaces combined with the many thousands of others around the city to create a gray winter pall that matched the general mood created by the economic depression of the 1930s. The heavily polluted air eventually dispersed when new laws required the use of anthracite or hard coal - a cleaner fuel - but the depression continued until the national economy was reinvigorated at the end of the decade by industrial mobilization for the Second World War. There were important issues and strong forces at work in the world as my friends and I in the neighborhood played soft ball when the weather was warm and touch football when it was cooler, sometimes in the dusty schoolyard before it was paved with asphalt and sometimes in the public parks or the narrow side streets that easily accommodated both us and the light vehicular traffic. The pre-suburban neighborhoods were compact, which meant there was no need for school buses or lunch rooms when both public and parochial schools were within easy walking distance of almost anywhere. Oddly, most of my friends had divorced parents, which made me suspect later in life that the financial turmoil created by the depression also had its domestic side-effects. I remind myself of those single parent homes and a shabbier time to avoid excessive nostalgia for a period that had its flaws. But as children, we were mainly unaware of the financial, political and military matters that troubled the adults. We had more immediate things on our minds.

In a way, that evening at Ernie's, ordinary by any standard, marked the dissolution of my university neighborhood, an area defined by the people and not the buildings around me, it was one of those neat divisions where one phase of your life ends and another begins, but the neatness and finality aren't apparent until some time later. I think Greg's death the following month began a slow process that eventually put a number of events and attendant recollections into a logical sequence for me. That sequence of events, I've come to realize, amounts to my life.

VEINTEDOS

I wasn't surprised to learn that Janet Joslyn had to a considerable extent invented herself. She'd created the person she wanted to be from the person she was, which in her case involved an elaborate, but not illegal, deception.

It was more than 20 years later, in the early 1970s, that Janet, by then in her mid 80s, died quietly of something called natural causes in a Manhattan apartment she'd shared for many years with a considerable art collection and three cats - Diego, David and Jose, named for the Mexican painters Rivera, Siqueiros and Orozco. The art collection turned out to be quite valuable while the cats, on the other hand, did not.

I learned of her death and, oddly enough, the rudiments of her life from a one-column obituary in The New York Times, a newspaper I received daily in the midwestern office where I worked at the time. The notice might have eluded me had it not been for the mildly eccentric habit I had of reading the paper back to front. I always read the obituaries before the front page to discover who had recently died and because the longer pieces - often good, short biographies - were usually more interesting than the news. When the essayist E.B. White died in 1985, for example, the paper ran a six column obit almost 15 inches deep with a three column picture of the author and his dachshund, Minnie, who sat on a desk staring at her master as he plunked away on an old, manual typewritter. Full of straight biographical as well as anecdotal material, the article neatly explained White's long, fond attachment to his wife, Katharine. Shortly after their marriage, White later said, "I soon learned that I had made no mistake in my choice of a wife. I was helping her pack an overnight bag one afternoon when she said, "Put in some tooth twine.' I knew then that a girl that called dental floss tooth twine was the girl for me" All the news that's fit to print and more.

Just as The Times told me about Katharine White and the tooth twine, it also told me that Janet Joslyn wasn't Janet Joslyn at all. Her obituary revealed she'd been born Ruby Smith in Oklahoma, and I later learned she was the only issue of a Cherokee mother and a white father whose successful but shady business dealings enabled him to send his bright daughter east to one of the name brand women's colleges. Ruby, or Janet, never went back and never looked back, apparently preferring her new identity, which she took on when she moved to New York after graduating with honors, to the half-breed stigma she'd endured throughout her Oklahoma childhood. She didn't realize it at the time, but her aboriginal heritage would probably have given her an exotic quality that most of her future associates, both personal and business, would have found either interesting or attractive and, in some cases, both. In time, that irony probably occurred to her.

Once in the city and probably financed with money from home, Janet soon met and made friends with a large circle of painters, sculptors, poets, musicians and art fanciers, some with considerable talent and some with none at all. She was good looking, overtly intelligent, pleasantly glib and an attentive listener, a quality that ensured her popularity with those in search of an audience. About this time, she had a short-lived affair with one of the most famous American painters of the early 20th century, a union that would have secured her place in art history had he not had the same kind of relationships with so many other women. In any event, Janet was not the kind of person, either then or later, who would let someone screw her into immortality.

Although not in the same way, she came to know many other prominent artists. She knew the Frenchman, Marcel Duchamp, who late in life was transformed into a naturalized American. Earlier, he had electrified- if that's the word-the New York art world when his painting, "Nude Descending a Staircase, No. 2", was exhibited at the 1913 Armory Show. Janet saw that show, now considered something of a landmark in the introduction of modern art to America, and I knew Janet, which is a little like saying I knew someone who heard Lincoln deliver the Gettysburg Address. It's like witnessing history once removed.

She also knew the photographer Alfred Stieglitz and his wife, Georgia O'Keeffe, who would one day repair to New Mexico and paint her way into very old age and worldwide recognition. And she knew Alfred's younger brother, Julius, who taught Chemistry at the University of Chicago for more than 40 years and wrote something called "Elements of Qualitative Chemical Analysis," which failed to make the best-seller lists of its time. Not that she knew these people very well, but they all knew her well enough to know who she was and what she did. And what she did was to open an art gallery that within 10 years would establish her reputation as someone who had an eye for new talent. The gallery secured her reputation within the art community, and she secured her financial independence, once and for all, through successive marriages to two wealthy men, one an investment banker and the other a senior executive with a large advertising agency. In both marriages, which tasted only a few years each and were terminated under amicable circumstances, she retained her adopted name. Janet was a civilized woman and she married civilized men, not, I'd wager, by accident.

I don't really know how her original interest in Mexico developed, perhaps through an attachment to the country's pre-Columbian or modern art. Or it may have been the beauty and great diversity of its land and culture, barely diminished by widespread poverty and political corruption. But whatever the initial attraction, her continuing attraction to the place was more than likely the result of an unresolved relationship with a young Mexican architect who died before the affair, as those things tend to do, fizzled out. She met him in Mexico City when she was in her early 40s and he was in his late 20s. They were together for only a few months when he went to Spain to fight for the republicans and simply disappeared. The assumption, of course, was that he died in the war, but that was pure conjecture. For all Janet knew, he could have met some Spanish tootsie and settled in for a long and distant life. Whatever his fate, Janet was left with the memory of a lover who'd not had sufficient time or opportunity to disillusion her. Trapped in that way, she probably transferred her love or affection or whatever it was to the country where she'd met this lost person. That's only a guess, but there's a limit to the information you can get from an obituary and other superficial sources.

Janet knew the important Mexican painters of her time, including Rufino Tamayo, whose work, some think, recalls the pre-Columbian art of the country. One night in Taxco, she told us that Tamayo, who was an Indian, would dress like an Indian peasant when he was in New York, and like an international diplomat when he was in Mexico City. For someone like Janet, who knew how to work a crowd, this behavior must have been especially revealing.

There was a persistent rumor while we were in Taxco that Janet was bedding Frank Mirabella, but I discounted it on the grounds she had too much taste and, despite her age, could have done a great deal better. In my opinion, anyone else would have been a great deal better. But, if nothing else, they both spoke fluent Spanish which, if the rumor was true, at least gave them one small measure of compatibility.

In the last decade of her life, Janet wrote a short book on the history of the Cherokees, which she published and distributed to some of her closest surviving friends. The book carefully avoided her personal history, but it never-the-less revealed, if you read it closely, that she had never lost touch with her origins and that, in all probability, her long deception had been conducted not out of shame but only as a device to avoid barriers to the goals she sought. And who - other than ethnocentric hardheads - would argue with success?

The Cherokees, she wrote in the book, were once the largest and single most important tribe in the southeastern United States, residing in mountainous areas of North and South Carolina, Georgia, Alabama and

Tennessee. By the 16th century, they had a settled, advanced culture supported by agriculture, and early in the 19th century they established themselves as The Cherokee Nation under a constitution with a principal chief, a senate and a house of representatives. Much of this progress - if that's what it was - was made possible with the invention of a Cherokee alphabet by an Indian scholar, silversmith, painter and warrior named Sequoya, who eventually took the name George Guess. His alphabet was approved by the Cherokee council in 1821 and was effective in teaching thousands of Indians to read and write. It also enabled the keeping of tribal records and the publication of tribal newspapers, which may have been a mixed blessing but it was certainly unique among the North American Indian tribes.

The discovery of gold in Cherokee Indian territory, not surprisingly, resulted in pressure by the whites to get their pink fingers on Indian lands. A treaty was extracted from a small part of the tribe, which bound the entire tribe to move beyond the Mississippi River within three years. Although the tribe overwhelmingly repudiated this document and the U.S. Supreme Court upheld the Nation's autonomy, the state of Georgia secured through one of its own courts an order for their removal, which was accomplished with military force. President Andrew Jackson refused to intervene and in 1838 a large part of the tribe was deported to the Indian Territory, a wilderness we now call Oklahoma. At that time, the corn wasn't as high as an elephant's eye.

Thousands of Cherokee men, women and children died on the march - now called "The Trail of Tears" - and from later hardships. But once in Oklahoma, the Cherokees created a capital as well as a school system and other trappings of civilization. During the American Civil War, their allegiance was divided and there were large groups serving on both sides. In 1892, when Janet was little more than a baby, the Cherokees sold their tribal territory, known as The Cherokee Strip, and disbanded as a tribe in 1906 to assume U.S. citizenship. A small number of Cherokees still live in western North Carolina, descendents of those slippery ones who successfully evaded removal or later returned from Oklahoma.

Janet conducted her annual Mexican workshops into the early 1960s, giving her an excuse to summer there and providing several hundred others with opportunities to either learn something about another culture or drink themselves half to death In a pleasant environment. Either way, the participants usually came away from the experience with an enduring admiration for the country and its peoples, unencumbered by any serious knowledge of its dictatorial government and venal politicians.

After she discontinued the workshops and long after she had disbanded her gallery, she settled into an old age that centered on occasional lunches with a few surviving friends and one-sided conversations with her cats, sometimes individually and sometimes collectively. Her health declined steadily in her final years, and her death arrived as no surprise to those who knew her near the end. When Janet died, the cats, who were also getting on in years by then, were dispersed among those few remaining friends.

VEINTETRES

Laura, who graduated an exclusive - which is another word for expensive - women's college in New Orleans, knew an older alumnus who lived the ex-patriot life in Taxco. The woman, Kate Walters, was something of a minor celebrity, a moderately successful popular fiction writer with a large local reputation as a hostess. She was also a large person with a broad, friendly face and a manner to match who liked to preside at dinners where the food was good, or better, and the conduct bordered on raucous. Laura, invited to one of Kate's dinners, wangled an invitation for me, no easy task given the popularity of these gatherings.

Kate was a truly sophisticated woman, the kind whose sophistication was so natural and obvious she didn't feel the need to prove anything to anyone. Not too far removed from high school and barely out of military service, there was little in the way of worldliness about me. But Kate, who insisted I use her given name, spoke and listened to me with the same relaxed intensity she provided guests who were famous, near famous, amusing, erudite or just plain strange, a particular virtue in her estimation.

A southerner whose accent had been largely obliterated by years of residence in a variety of cities and several countries, Kate had been married four or five times to husbands who continued to hold her in a fair amount of esteem for her unfailing good humor, generosity of spirit and, I'd guess, for the recollection of great times. She was a woman who knew how to dump a spouse, just as she knew how to give a memorable party. Her husbands, I was told, had not been in the least bit similar. They had not been carbon copies of prior mistakes. One had been a wealthy American businessman and another a titled middle European. Her last husband, divorced several years earlier, had been a Mexican painter at least 20 years her junior. Her appetites went well beyond good food and had not yet been fully satisfied, a condition that could have accounted for her remarkable tolerance of bizarre, sometimes aberrant, behavior in others. But mostly, I think, she had a keen intelligence and a well developed sense of humor that enabled her to take things, good and bad, as they came, and to extract as much enjoyment from life as she could.

The guests that night were more sedate than usual, including an ancient, long-since retired U.S. naval officer and his wife, gracefully approaching dotage, and a tall sculptress who lived in the nearby mountains and who had arrived with two huge Great Danes that someone said went everywhere with her, which was barely anywhere since she seldom left her remote home. The dogs settled in comfortably with about a half dozen other guests who either lived in Taxco or were passing through on their way north or south. One of them was the former wife of a famous American playwright and another was a quiet European man, perhaps in his early 30s, who someone described as the visiting son of one of Kate's ex-husbands.

There was also a middle-aged surgeon from Mexico City, balding and with an emerging waistline, whose last operation, I suspected, had been the bloodless penetration of his companion, a large-breasted young woman in her late teens. There were two others - a man and a woman, perhaps married - who lived in Taxco and ran some kind of commercial enterprise. They were a relaxed, straight-forward couple who mingled well with the other guests and may well have been there for that very reason.

In her usually expansive mood after dinner - which followed cocktails and included a number of wine courses - Kate told us about a party she gave in a house where she once lived in the mountains well removed from town. A particularly violent storm developed, washing out the steep, narrow road to the main highway, and also disrupting the electric power that wasn't all that reliable under the best conditions. The guests, about a dozen of them, had done a good deal of drinking before the lights went out, and the introduction of candles only enhanced the generally festive mood. As the party gained in intensity, Kate said, someone noticed despite the flickering light that one of the older guests was seated in a chair, his chin slumped on his chest and his arms hanging limply extended, palms up, at his sides. Given the circumstances, he could well have been drunk, but his posture had that distinctive quality that suggested something more permanent. And, indeed, the old fart was dead as the famous doornail, victim of what was later diagnosed or professionally presumed a massive coronary thrombosis.

The corpse, once known to the world as Benito Juarez Morales or Benny to his friends, had been a minor player in the 1910 revolution that traded a repressive but efficient dictatorship for seven years of revolution and civil war, which produced a great deal; of bloodshed and ruin in a country that had been uncharacteristically stable for nearly 35 years. That stability had largely been the work of Porfirio Diaz, who seized power in 1876 and held control of the country until the revolution that brought him down broke out only a decade into the new century. Diaz resigned and escaped to France, leaving a series of successors to preside over the chaos. All this instability threatened American investment and the U.S. sent punitive expeditions into Mexico in 1914 and 1916 when General Pershing fruitlessly chased Pancho Villa all over the place in what became a short rehearsal for Yankee participation in the First World War. Despite the adoption in 1917 of a new constitution that gave Mexico a congress and elected president, the nation's progress through the first half of the 20th century generally failed to achieve the revolutionary ideals that had been the justification for so much political and military activity since 1821 when after 300 years the Mexicans got rid of the Spaniards.

Only a few of Kate Walter's guests were aware of the dead man's revolutionary past, a record that was based mainly on his own vague and generalized claims, and rumors that may well have originated with the same source. But he looked the part with his fierce eyes, leathery complexion and full white mustache, curled at the ends, and most of those who knew him accepted his revolutionary past under the assumption the issue, one way or the other, would have no lasting effect on anything. It was a civilized attitude, I thought, that did them credit.

Kate thought so, too, and said as much. She liked Benny for his own qualities, but also used him as a kind of prop for her parties. He was a little like one of those old cigar store wooden Indians that didn't say anything but drew attention to itself as the result of its strangeness and imposing stature. He usually sat somewhere off to the side, chain-smoking cheap little cigars and letting an occasional rumor about his past swirl, like the smoke, about him.

The storm had washed out the road and shut down the electrical supply at a time when the state of technology in the region made improbable any communication with anyone in town. There were not only no cellular phones, regular telephone lines had not yet been strung to this area. That meant the corpse would remain in the house until the road was reopened, an event not likely to occur until the storm abated and someone, probably by sheer accident, noticed that no one had come off the mountain in some time. And there were many mountains in the area, all in the same washed-out condition.

The storm, drained by its own fury, spent itself before the night was over but the road remained closed for three days. Kate and her guests, meanwhile, dealt with the body in a manner that was reasonable, if not ingenious, given the tack of alternatives. They lay Benny in relative state on a large couch in the main room and placed candles, which they kept lit in ceremonial fashion around him on the stone floor. Someone folded his arms on his chest and he lay there on his back for three days, eyes open and staring blankly at the timbered ceiling, as he slowly decomposed and the party went on around him.

VEINTEQUATRO

As an educated Mexican of Spanish descent - with all that implied in terms of pride and, perhaps, a little arrogance - Tony deeply resented the United States, but that resentment was directed more at the government or, possibly, some abstract imperialistic concept rather than the Yankees who passed through his bar in a continuous stream. He took the gringos one by one and either liked or disliked them, or in most cases remained indifferent, based entirely on their human qualities and nothing more In conversations with anyone from the United States, he usually held his opinions about their country to himself out of an inbred courtesy that went far beyond simple politeness. He was, despite his relative youth, a gentleman of the really old school, which meant he was courteous to a fault unless you crossed him.

Tony and I were only casual acquaintances, friends in a tenuous and temporary manner, but early in our relationship I recognized some of the things that defined his character. He had what Laura called "charm" and I saw as "style", but the quality, while not the least bit phony, was superficial. Tony maintained it as a barrier against those who would penetrate his deep reserve, which was altogether private and personal. And while I could barely imagine what was buried in that reserve (and wouldn't try), I suspected that he simply thought most things beyond the really trivial were best kept to himself.

Given that assessment of Tony, I was surprised one night late in the summer when he drew me into a discussion, if that's what it was, of the ambivalent relations between the United States and Mexico. The subject more or less seeped into the conversation, initiated by some forgotten remarks by one of us as we sat at a window table in his bar with Laura and Betty each sipping something with lime. The women had drifted into their own conversation, either out of real interest or the desire to avoid ours, when Tony, in his quiet way, leaned back in his chair and delivered what amounted to a long lecture. We weren't in any kind of disagreement and the lecture wasn't, I felt, directed at me so much as it was meant to organize thoughts that had been assembling in his mind over a long period of time. I was merely a sounding board, a prop that kept him from delivering his message to the thin, mountain air. As I listened to him I realized he was a more thoughtful man than I would have guessed and that his feelings about his country's history and future were, I judged, intense and sincere. I wondered if he had always been this way or if the Spanish war had anything to do with his historical introspection.

Half jokingly, Tony began by telling me that his countrymen used "gringo" because it was the only applicable word for someone from the United States. Everyone from the top of Canada to Tierre del Fuego, he said, was an American and he wasn't going to grant us an exclusive right to the title. Even the term Yankee was inappropriate, he went on, because he wasn't fool enough to apply that word to someone from Georgia or South Carolina. His reference to those two southern states was a little embarrassing to me, revealing, as it did, that he knew more about U.S. geography than I did about the Mexican kind. I would have been hard pressed at the time to identify two states in his country.

The word "gringo," I knew, was a disparaging way for Latinos to describe outlanders, usually Americans and sometimes Englishmen. I later learned from a dictionary that it's similar to the Greek word "griego," which means "stranger." Oh, well, I remember thinking, I've been called worse.

"Your President Polk," Tony began in earnest referring to James K. Polk, who in the interest of U.S. expansion initiated the Mexican-American War in the 1840s, "essentially stole California and New Mexico from my country and confirmed the earlier theft of Texas by a band of barely literate renegades." Polk, he failed to mention, had been the first, if you'll pardon the term, American president to pledge himself to a single term in office and then in that short period accomplish pretty much what he set out to do. Unfortunately for Mexico, what he set out to do was divest them of vast territories. Fortunately for Polk, he got the job done in his single term. He died three months after leaving office and was succeeded by Zachary Taylor, who had commanded the Army of the Rio Grande that defeated the Mexican forces under the general, Antonio Lopez de Santa Anna, at Buena Vista early in 1847, ending the war in northern Mexico. By most accounts as well as the results, Taylor was a fine military commander and a lousy president who, through a stroke of national luck, died a year and a half into his presidential tenure, which wasn't soon enough to suit Tony. He felt the same way about General Winfield Scott, who also defeated Santa Anna in a series of battles that culminated in the American occupation of Mexico City. Scott, too, ran for the American presidency but lost, which probably explains how he managed to live five years past his retirement.

They, Tony said, referring to some individualized concept he had of 19th century Americans, called Taylor "Old Rough-and-Ready" and referred to Scott as "Old Fuss and Feathers." What in hell does that mean? he wanted to know. I tried to explain that the nicknames were meant to describe their personalities, respectfully and affectionately, in a simpler time, but he merely shook his head to indicate the names were just plain silly. I suppose he would have thought otherwise had they called Santa Anna "Old Hot Tamale" or something along those lines.

Beaten decisively in the Mexican-American War, just as he was defeated by Sam Houston at San Jacinto in the earlier Texas rebellion, Santa Anna was one resilient old duck. In a long and turbulent career, he led revolts against three different Mexican governments, served as president or provisional president of the country on several occasions and once as dictator. He was deposed, exiled and recalled a couple of times and managed during his life to live in Cuba, Venezuela, St. Thomas and the United States, finally returning to Mexico where he died in his early 80s. At the end, Santa Anna was poverty-stricken and largely forgotten, but he outlived Polk, Taylor and Scott.

I think Tony thought of Santa Anna as just another politician, but he was a Mexican politician which, for Tony, mitigated to some extent his extravagant shortcomings. Mainly, Tony resented the naked aggression that the United States used to wrest much of its western territories from Mexico. That same aggressiveness, he said, had been employed from time to time, particularly in Latin America, by a nation that likes to preach freedom to the rest of the world. America had long tinkered in Mexican affairs and it was high time it stopped, he was saying when Laura interrupted, leaning in my direction and putting a hand on my arm. "Betty's going to have a baby," she revealed. The news was timely, not that I cared much about Betty's baby but because I'd heard enough historical fault-finding for one evening. My national pride hadn't been bruised as much as my attention span, which had been beaten half to death. "When's the little gringo due?" I inquired slyly, knowing I was running a small risk that Tony might be offended by my simple attempt to redirect the conversation. Instead, he was amused. "I'm sorry," he said, smiling his hostly smile. "I've been a terrible bore, but I know how to rectify the situation. He meant he was going to provide a round of drinks, which he did by raising an arm and snapping a couple of fingers. When the drinks arrived, I proposed a toast. "Here's to little Nigel," I said, raising my glass. This time, Tony laughed out loud. "Fat chance," he replied. Laura and Betty took small, ceremonial sips of their drinks and, not knowing or caring what we were talking about, returned to their earlier discussion. Tony and I went on to talk about more recent matters and it was soon evident, to my great relief, that he'd forgotten the late President Polk and those dead generals.

VEINTECINCO

The summer passed swiftly, composed of days occupied by drawing and painting, either on a sun-swept terrace at the Humboldt or in a variety of locations that suited our individual fancies The workshop discipline, set on a scale, ranged from lax to limpid, which suited me perfectly. I had come to Mexico mainly to come to Mexico, and had no illusions about my abilities as a painter. As far as I was concerned, the workshop could have been a school for automobile mechanics.

Laura and I spent one particularly pleasant afternoon in late summer making sketches in an ancient cemetery where the faded facades of once colorful headstones contrasted with fresh flowers that proved there were people who remembered or respected the past. Or both. I still have an evocative oil sketch of the place given to me by Laura that afternoon. It wasn't representative of her best work - which is probably why she was willing to part with it - but I've kept it all these years as other possessions have either been lost or left behind in the course of many moves.

Laura not only didn't give her work away readily, she could barely be persuaded to sell it. She reminded me of a young sculptor from Germany I met many years later at a Milwaukee gallery where his work was on display. I purchased a model he'd made for a large public piece with the understanding he'd retain the work for a month before it was delivered to me. He needed the model for some obscure reason, and I had lived my life to that point without it. But when several months elapsed without delivery of the piece - which I'd paid for - or an explanation from anyone, I called the gallery where I learned they knew nothing of the arrangement. I then called the sculptor, who apologized in the most profuse and abject manner and promised to personally deliver it to me the next day. He not only delivered the model but explained in halting English that he had great difficulty relinquishing any of his work, even the large ones. Unfortunately, he said, not using that exact word, he had a wife and five small children and needed the money. Laura didn't need the money, but she had the same kind of attachment to her work.

There were during that summer a continuous succession of dinners, parties and other indulgences. It was only five years after the second major war of the half century had ended, and most of the people I knew wanted to have a good time. They thought we were through with that sort of thing for a while and were surely surprised by Korea and, later, Viet Nam. Some of my friends, called up for military service in Korea, were especially surprised as I idled the summer away in Taxco.

The dissolution of the workshop in late summer was made formal with a self-contained fiesta, hosted by Janet and held in Tony's cantina. She had hired a small band, one of those Mexican ensembles made up of guitars and horns that wandered from table to table and played loudly until the last dog was dead. The musicians were dressed in black suits with sliver buttons and massive belts that had, with one exception, the word "Mexico" prominently engraved on the equally massive buckles. The one exception was a guitar player whose buckle read "Boston." Someone in our group that evening asked one of the musicians about the Bostonian, and he shrugged and said simply: "Gringo." The joke, I think, was on us.

As parties go, this was a pretty good one, building in numbers and volume as the evening and night wore on and gradually thinning out until it expired of inertia In the early hours of the following morning. The guests were mainly workshop members, supplemented by Janet's friends from the community and other far-flung places. Laura and I sat from time to time at a table with Mary Beth, Marie, Jack and several other transients, and also visited various individuals and couples, particularly Tony and the pregnant Betty, at the bar. The noise that evening - a combination of voices, outside fireworks and a band that played "Guadalajara" until we wished they'd go there - soon made most of us hoarse from trying to make ourselves heard above the din. I recall, too, there was little breeze that evening and a pall of cigarette smoke hung in the air despite the open windows. This smoke was from Mexican cigarettes, which those of us who smoked had adopted over the summer for lack of an American alternative.

I remained relatively sober that evening, sipping my drinks judiciously to avoid a repetition of my drunken behavior earlier that summer. Since most of the others didn't have prior humiliations to trouble them, they drank with varying degrees of abandon and many of them were at least mildly stoned by mid-night. Some of them stumbled off into the night, saying their final goodbyes to anyone who'd listen, and others remained to get really fried. I noticed later in the evening that Mary Beth and Francis were apparently having some kind of disagreement, although I didn't and don't have the foggiest notion of what it was about. "Francis," I heard Mary Beth say, "you don't need an analyst, you need a hard kick in the ass." Jack, sitting nearby, had passed out but, given his normal reclusion, nobody had noticed.

I had wanted to talk to Laura privately on our last night together in Mexico, an opportunity I didn't get because we remained at the party until it was too late for anything but sleep. We had to travel the next day and we probably realized there wasn't anything that either one of us might say that would alter the situation. I wasn't in any position to propose anything, and Laura, I'm sure, liked me, but not as a permanent attachment to her life. We said good night at the Humboldt, had coffee together the next morning and went our separate ways.

I took my little Chevrolet and, alone, headed north along that interminable two-lane highway. I remember trying to persuade Laura only hours before to let me drive her to Dallas on my way home, but we both knew that wasn't a good idea. The women who had come south with me in June had found another way home in August, which may have inspired my offer to Laura. More than likely, I simply didn't want her to return to the family fold. I knew her as an individual apart from her husband and daughters, and had a hard time accepting a more complicated and extended set of circumstances. Later, I realized that others before me - many others - had made the same mistake.

Once on the road, I pushed the car and myself relentlessly through the mountains, tropics and desert, stopping only to eat or sleep when it was absolutely necessary. My cash reserves were low, I missed Laura and, while I was still in Mexico, I couldn't get a damn thing on the car radio worth listening to as the miles zipped by and time stood still. I turned it off for good when "Guadalajara" reached me from some low wattage station at the edge of civilization.

The trip was tiring but uneventful until I reached the outskirts of Neuvo Laredo, just across the Rio Grande River from Texas, where one of my tires blew late on a very hot afternoon. I replaced it with a spare, muttering words I wouldn't repeat in a motorcycle bar, and, drenched in August sweat, drove across the bridge into the United States, where I discovered the country had gone on a partial war-time economic footing. There wasn't a new tire to be had in the whole bloody town, but I managed with most of my remaining money to find an over-priced used one to replace the spare. That purchase ensured that I wouldn't eat or sleep very much until I reached home.

I returned to St. Louis to learn that Greg had been dead since June, long since buried, and to wonder what Laura's life was like in Dallas. And, possibly for the first time, I began to realize there was nothing permanent about life. There's nothing profound in that realization, I realize, and it took me a long time, 22 years, to even approach the subject. I'm sure I might have managed it earlier had my Marine Corps service been during the war when young men I knew might have been killed. But introspection has never been one of my primary concerns, and that's been a great comfort to me over the years. I'm not one of those people who needs to ponder the impenetrable. I prefer to remember the surface events, particularly the good ones, and leave the underlying meaning to anyone foolish enough to think there is any. Call me shallow, but don't call me for church.

Given that attitude, it seems pointless to wish Greg a peaceful and eternal rest. But the United States, I've heard, is a free country where they don't usually throw you in jail for contradictions. And since there's nothing to lose and I didn't have an opportunity to say goodbye, I have a few parting words for my friend.

Greg, old boy:

I hope your death was relatively painless, which is to say I hope your lights went out instantly when that speeding assemblage of metal crushed your unsuspecting bone and tissue. I regret your death so young, mostly for my own selfish reasons. I was really curious to know how you'd turn out. You were one crazy son-of-a-bitch as a young man, and I wanted to know if you could have sustained that quality into maturity. Perhaps.

Anyway, there are those of us who remember you, and we do it fondly.

TWENTY-SIX

As I drove west from New Orleans bound for Dallas on Christmas Day, the radio news reports from Korea were uniformly depressing. General MacArthur, whose United Nations forces had pushed the North Korean army all the way back to the Chinese-Manchurian border in October, had seriously underestimated Chinese intentions and military strength. The General surely had second thoughts as thousands of enemy troops swarmed over the frontier and by early December had driven the good guys out of Pyongyang, North Korea's capital, and gone on to shove UN soldiers back south over ground they had only recently covered going in the other direction.

I didn't know it as the Louisiana countryside rolled past my car window, but the United Nations would mount a counter-offensive in late January and another the following June, gradually regaining enough lost ground to establish an effective stalemate. As I headed toward Texas in response to an invitation from Laura, who had passed me off to her family as a friend from the "Mexican workshop" there seemed little chance the Chinese multitudes could be stopped any time soon. My patriotic depression brought on by this turn of events was compounded by a financial one caused by the loss on Christmas Eve of half my cash to a 17-year-old Bourbon

Street stripper who had neatly slipped the money from a wallet in a jacket I had carelessly put on a barstool next to her. She had joined me, without invitation, between shows and I bought her a drink. She told me she had only recently come to New Orleans from a carnival job of some kind, and that she'd run away from a rural Georgia home less than a year earlier to escape an abusive father and a ton of sisters and brothers. She'd learned a lot, I later thought, in those few months.

I left the joint when she returned to work and only discovered the loss when I tried to buy myself a drink a few minutes later at a nearby bar. The stripper had not taken all my money, probably for lack of opportunity, and I was able to pay for the current drink and ponder my alternatives. I had decided that any attempt to recover the lost cash would only put me in conflict with some big, surly bouncer when another stripper - this one called "The Panther Girl" on a prominent sign outside the entrance- sat down next to me and proposed that I buy her a drink. I doubt there was much in life that would have surprised this woman, but I don't think she expected me to tell her to go fuck herself, which is precisely what I did. She fled me like the plague and, presumably, went back to panthering.

The Bourbon Street experience made me feel like the ultimate mark, the world's principal victim. It was as if someone had put a sign on my back - visible to every thief on earth - that identified me as a moron or worse. I knew that almost anyone could be conned, but it took a particular kind of dope to let a 17-year-old girl just off the farm do it. I took some consolation in the thought she might have lied about her age.

I had put the matter and New Orleans behind me the next day when I made the long drive to Dallas where I was reunited with Laura and met her husband, Curtis, and two daughters, seven-year-old Clarissa and five-year-old Sally. I had known that Laura's circumstances were privileged, but the extent of that privilege surprised me. I had thought of her background as upper middle class, but now learned that the family resources were a good deal greater. Her home, set on a dozen acres, was large, rambling and understated in the manner I have come to associate with long-term affluence. She described the house as "Louisiana style" for some architectural reason I never understood, but accepted out of deference to the fact she'd gone to school in New Orleans. There was nothing newly rich or flashy about the place or, for that matter, the family. Curtis, who was tall, pink-cheeked and conservative down to his loafers, was a perfect host, although I only saw him on two occasions during my three-day visit and I had the distant suspicion he wasn't entirely thrilled to see me. On the other hand, the girls seemed to like me, possibly because they knew I had not been an adult long enough for it to have seriously affected my judgment. The younger one, Sally, was especially attentive, describing in excessive detail the recent production of Dickens' "A Christmas Carol" she'd just seen for the first time. I listened with feigned attentiveness because I had no choice in the matter. She was an insistent but charming little character. To my great relief her sister was more distant, although friendly to this intruder from some unfamiliar place. They were both pretty - as many little girls tend to be - but Clare, unlike Sally, resembled her father. Sally probably bore his genes, but it gave me some latent pleasure to suspect Laura might have produced her with assistance from another man. Curtis, it seemed, didn't exactly thrill me, either.

I was lodged in a small guest house at the back of their property in a dense grove of southern pines. The house, not surprisingly, was occasionally used for guests, but it mainly served as Laura's studio, a retreat from family and social affairs where she could paint, read or ponder whatever bright, attractive, indulged southern women ponder. During those few days, Laura took me to lunch at their country club, dinner at her favorite restaurant, and we spent odd times just talking in the guest house. Laura, Curtis and I had dinner in the main house on the final night of my visit, and they retired early to accommodate a business meeting he had to attend the next morning. There was also the very real possibility he'd seen enough of me by that time.

Not tired and unwilling to tell them I wasn't finished with the evening, I clandestinely took my car in search of some night life in the midst of that suburban wilderness. I either didn't know or had forgotten that local liquor laws would make the search exceedingly difficult, but I finally blundered across what we once called a road house, in this case a low-lying, concrete block building with big, front windows illuminated by red and blue neon beer signs on both sides of the entrance. It looked like heaven to me.

Inside, however, it looked more like every other dingy little dump I'd seen in my short, saloon-happy life. The place was mostly dark and what light there was came from an old juke box and a further assortment of beer signs behind the bar and on the walls of a perfectly square room. There were several men seated up and down the bar, which was attended by a large, beefy chap in a soiled white apron, and a lone couple, male and female, sat at a table just across the small dance floor.

The smelt of old beer clung to the pace like sweat on your brow, if you'll pardon a lousy simile.

I sat down on a stool at one end of the bar and waited for the bartender to come take my order, which he did in his own good time. As I sat there, thinking about nothing in particular, the rising sound of words spoken in anger captured my attention. The words came from the couple, who were having what soon turned out to be a considerable difference of opinion. She was a scrawny, little twit and he didn't look that good in an old, white shirt and worn-out jeans. "You bastard," she kept saying and he responded in kind, although I caught only his nasty intent and not the exact terms. Soon, the others at the bar were watching the argument which meant they knew what was happening when the woman went to the juke box, inserted a coin and walked directly over to the man at the far end of the bar from me. "You want to dance?" she asked, as the machine started to play "Tennessee Waltz" and her boyfriend glared in their direction. The man at the bar quickly declined and she went on to the next customer "Want to dance?" she asked again. About that time, I thought I could predict the sequence of events. All the men between that troublesome woman and me would surely decline her invitations, and she'd arrive in my vicinity just as her equally troublesome boyfriend came over to vent his rage or frustration or whatever it was that made those veins pop out at his temples. Actually, the little fart didn't look all that intimidating, but I'd come there for a beer and, perhaps, some idle conversation, not a fight. And conventional wisdom tells anyone who will listen to stay out of domestic disputes.

There's a good chance those two losers would have converged on me had it not been for one of the neatest manifestations of poetic justice I've ever seen. Just as that goofy woman was about to ask the next man to dance, the bartender zipped around the bar. I thought he was going to deliver a warning, but he grabbed her upper arms from behind with what I saw were very large hands, lifted the woman off the floor and carried her now rigid body swiftly to the door. He looked directly at the boyfriend, who was half his size, and said: "One word out of you and I'll break your ugly face." With that, he opened the door and not too gently deposited the woman outside. She hadn't, meanwhile, said a word or moved a muscle. The boyfriend, who had seen the ease with which the woman had been lifted off her feet, followed her out the door once the bartender had cleared the way. The rest of us were silent for a moment and then, one by one, we began to clap our hands in appreciation. I finished my beer and left, knowing the evening could have nothing better to offer.

Laura awakened me early the next morning after Curtis had left for his business meeting, and we made love in the guest house before I motored out of her life. She seemed less passionate than usual and I correctly surmised the reason. She'd made love to Curtis earlier that morning and her union with me was only a courtesy gesture. She said as much, assuming I'd understand. Understand what? That she'd screwed her husband, practically in my presence, and showed absolutely no remorse, I slowly realized I was being unreasonable, although there's no law against it. There should be, but there isn't. We managed to part friends, and I'm grateful for that to this day.

I never saw Laura again, but I spoke with her on the phone 20 years later. On a business trip to Dallas, I tried unsuccessfully to find her number in the telephone directory. I assumed she had either moved, died or was unlisted. I was wrong on all three counts. The truth was revealed to me by Mary Seth, who was listed and who in response to a call joined me for dinner at my hotel. She explained that Laura had remarried many years before and still maintained a home in Dallas, among other places. The other places turned out to be Mexico and India, with India a concession to her second husband who just liked it there. Laura told me as much when I called her the next day. She also described herself as "a gray-haired, old lady," which really meant that she'd aged well. Our conversation included an invitation to lunch with her, which I couldn't accept. My flight north left in a couple of hours and for unremembered reasons I had to be on it.

I regret that I missed the lunch, just as I'm sorry that I again lost track of both Laura and Mary Beth after that trip. I don't know if our relationships could have been sustained, but I suspect that an occasional letter, even years apart, would have maintained a connection with them, which also would have been a connection with Greg and all the others I associated with that summer in and out of Mexico.

TWENTY-SEVEN

I gave little thought to the future in the summer of 1950. The approaching autumn, as far as I was concerned, was a distant prospect, too far away for recognition let alone contemplation. I was, of course, eventually to discover that the future - if one is lucky enough to survive - soon emerges from the present like a butterfly from a cocoon. Not a difficult concept, really, but one, like others, that eluded me for some time.

As it turned out my future was destined to be more extensive than I expected when I was 22. This unanticipated longevity on my part may have been made possible by the plethora of medical advances in the second half of the 20th century, family genetics or just plain dumb luck. Whatever the cause, I appreciate the effect.

Early in 1951, I sold my car and used the money for a ticket to Europe aboard the original Queen Mary, an elegant Cunard liner that had hauled thousands of Allied troops around during the second big war. I landed after a stormy North Atlantic crossing from New York to Cherbourg, where ships sunk as a result of the war still clogged the harbor, making it necessary for smaller boats to ferry passengers ashore from the huge trans-Atlantic vessels. From there, I took a crowded boat train to Paris, arriving late at night with less fluency in French than I had in Spanish and only the name of a cheap, left bank hotel scribbled on a scrap of paper by a young Canadian woman I'd met on the Queen Mary. She was a student at Cambridge who, when I disembarked, remained on the ship for its Channel crossing to England.

The same dumb luck that transported me into maturity got me safely to the hotel and through two months in France and England with only $200, a pittance even then, and a return ticket to the United States. I managed to stretch my dollars with what were probably illegal black market currency exchanges that got me more francs than I could have expected from American Express or some other reputable institution. I didn't realize at the time that some sharp operator could and may have pawned counterfeit francs off on me, but the local money worked and the gendarmes left me alone. More dumb luck, I suspect.

I returned to the U.S. in late spring aboard the Queen Mary's sister ship, Queen Elizabeth, and took a bus from New York to St. Louis, arriving home with less capital than when I'd returned from Mexico. Penury was getting to be a habit I did little to avoid, leaving a week later for California where I visited Jim Kelly and took that exhilarating ambulance ride through the streets of Oakland when he conked his head on the beer hall floor. The balance of 1951 - which extended from late spring to the end of the year - is largely a massive blank, but early in 1952 I met the young woman I would marry a few months later. I met Ann at the Mardi Gras, not the pre-Lenten orgy in New Orleans but a bar by the same name in south St. Louis that was characterized, especially on

Friday nights, by a crush of young people thirsting for more drink than many of them could handle and other forms of short-term gratification. We were married that summer and I returned to the University of Missouri at Columbia, where we remained until I conned them out of a liberal arts degree a couple of years later. At this point, I wish I could tell you I went on to study medicine, became a distinguished pediatric neurosurgeon and developed a widely employed vascular device that has saved the lives of countless patients, mainly innocent children with angelic faces whose parents worship the ever-loving ground I trod. Not so, and why are you not surprised?

The truth - if that's what you want - is that I went to work as a reporter for a small, daily newspaper in the state capital, an occupation I little respected and a publication where the editorial opinion would have been greatly improved had it merely been stupid and ill-informed. Through some kind of perverted industry I'd accidentally developed at the University, I won a small measure of respect from the elderly woman who owned this small-time, but extraordinarily profitable, communications empire, which included radio and television stations. Actually, the respect was won when I volunteered to do a Saturday afternoon radio news broadcast. My willingness to work without pay, which I did to gain some vague thing called experience, gladdened her ancient capitalist heart and she later offered me a news position at the television station when the incumbent broadcaster abruptly resigned to take a job in what he described as "a major, north-central market". At first, I thought he was going to work in a Milwaukee grocery store.

My early performances on the six o'clock news were ghastly, something that suggested a gibbering idiot one moment and a catatonic moron the next. And I didn't improve much over the next several years despite a work schedule that made me do it five times a week, including those holidays that didn't fall on weekends. I reported more murders, robberies, automobile accidents, floods, fires, elections, parades and other trivialities than weaker men could have endured. To put it another way, I never became a competent broadcaster, but I did become a minor local celebrity whose contacts, some of them political, enabled me to parlay that silly job into a gubernatorial appointment as the assistant director of a small, largely useless, state government agency. I got the appointment because someone suspected I might be able to write speeches for the governor, one of the state's great political characters and a splendidly effective stump or extemporaneous speaker. Unfortunately, he couldn't read a speech to save his ass, which made my job interesting in one particular respect. When he delivered one of my speeches, I never knew which words of more than two syllables he'd mispronounce. But this minor insufficiency didn't alter the governor's unshakable self-confidence, and he kept me on until I managed to get a public relations job in Chicago with one of the major airline companies. My new boss, another character, once worked for the Associated Press when a decent wire service correspondent wrote terse copy and drank some form of alcohol to excess. This one worked hard, fueled only by a daily glass of tomato juice for breakfast, a bowl of soup for lunch and a half dozen highballs before dinner. He once told me he'd give anything to be constipated, if only for a little while. The source of his problem was immediately apparent to me, but I don't think he had a clue.

I soon tired of the airline business, mainly because my boss traveled me half to death throughout the year I worked for him. He'd dispatch me to Indianapolis, Louisville, Detroit or some other mid-western city on a whim or to New York for long, tedious staff meetings he wanted to personally avoid. And since the airline had a policy - admirable from the customer's point of view - that wouldn't let an employee displace a paying passenger on its flights, I carried out this heavy traveling schedule as a chronic stand-by. That meant I was constantly at an airline gate, worn out and anxious to go home, as planes full of what the company called "revenue passengers" left without me. Screw that I thought and probably said out loud before I resigned and returned to work for the governor, who took me back because his administrative assistant, my friend, convinced him I'd not do any irreparable damage.

This time I was given a long title that meant absolutely nothing and a comfortable but obscure office in the state capitol building, where I again wrote speeches and other long-forgotten things when I needed to, and wandered around the marble halls and other places to gather information from various sources when the mood struck me. All this wandering made me a veritable compendium of knowledge related to the state of public health, welfare, highways, agriculture, prisons and education, both higher and otherwise, as well as most of the concerns of government at that level. I knew more about the swine brucellosis program than any city boy needed to know, and more about the state budget than the average legislator. It was a pretty interesting job with a single, important flaw for anyone who sought tenure. At the time, the governor was constitutionally limited to a single term, which had less than a year to go when I decided to get out of public life before the approaching elections did it for me. I subsequently returned to what some have called the "private sector" - which is almost as private as the floor of the New York Stock Exchange - and worked in various positions over the next quarter century for three different companies that shared several traits. These corporations did what they did in a variety of countries, made dozens of different products, mostly from metal, and were run by essentially decent but ordinary men who apparently came to think they'd risen to their over-paid positions through a combination of divine intervention and a knowledge of accounting. I knew otherwise, but kept my mouth shut.

One of the companies, for some reason I never knew, once published a Spanish language automobile parts catalog in Belgium for use in Latin America. One of the principal words on the cover was "Spanish," which in that language is "Espanol." By mistake, "espinaca," which mean spinach in Spanish, was unintentionally substituted for Espanol. The error led a couple of young smart-asses in the company's international division to reply to almost any question in Spanish with "No hablo espinaca" which, as you surely know by now, means: I don't speak spinach.

The only point of the anecdote is that large organizations make small mistakes, usually a lot of small mistakes. Large companies, governments, military organizations and the like are prone to screw up. I marvel that they function at all, let alone show profits, pass laws and win wars. Unlike the organizations that employed me, I didn't make many mistakes, but I marvel, once again, that I managed all those years of work without once getting fired, not for incompetence but for pig-headed obstinacy. I was often an insubordinate pain-in-the-ass to those above me on the organization chart, exhibiting behavior I never would have tolerated from those who worked under me. I didn't realize it at the time, of course, especially when I'd slam the door shut as I entered a superior's office and began the conversation with a "Goddamit, Bill" or something in that less than conciliatory vein. There were at least several occasions when I deserved firing, but I not only skirted those deserts but usually got generous salary increases on a regular schedule. Still more dumb luck.

I used to joke that I'd like to get canned because what I did wasn't fit work for a grown man. I carried that comment from job to job, which makes me now think that, perhaps, the grown man wasn't fit for the work. That work may have been devoid of any great purpose, but it was mildly interesting from time to time and I had the good fortune to run my small domains free of close scrutiny from those long-suffering but tolerant bosses of mine. The point, if I can find it, is that meaningless work can be amusing, which doesn't cure cancer or feed the hungry, but it will get an average person comfortably through life... unless they've glimpsed something along the way they like better.

I think I glimpsed something in Mexico that summer that I liked better, but I don't know to this day exactly what it was. I only know that I sensed another path at a time before I acquired the self-discipline that got me through the university and a succession of reasonably good jobs. I wonder if the same discipline, applied to other efforts, could have given me a more productive life in terms of real achievement and, possibly, on a broader geographic and cultural scale. I, unlike Greg, was given the time to do whatever I could manage. The question is: Could I have managed more?

The probable answer is no. I am, after all, a self-centered pig whose gone through life, like that summer in Mexico, from one indulgence to another. On the positive side, I haven't killed anyone, yet, and I'm uniformly kind to children and small animals, as long as they don't bite. I am also tidy, loyal, debt-free and only use bad language when it's absolutely appropriate. In other words, I've probably done as well as I could given my abilities and, more importantly, disposition, and the summer In Mexico is a pleasant memory and nothing more. And even Greg - had he lived and made something of himself - would have eventually disappeared into the endless future like everyone and everything else.

I now look at life as I look at art, which is a view that wouldn't satisfy those who insist on eternal verities. I don't see any deep, underlying purpose in art or life, only color, composition and sometimes, texture. But there's a lot to be said for good color, composition and texture, which brings me to my real point. And not a page too soon.

What's done is done and we can't do a damn thing about it. We can't wish it, pray it or beat it into something else, no matter how hard we try. The memory of that summer in Mexico - which mainly invokes my recollections of Laura and many other things I had not known until then - and Greg - who reminds me of other people in my distant past - are good memories I intend to enjoy, just as I plan to forget the bad ones and be grateful for plain, dumb luck.

THREE DRUNKEN SAILORS, AN AFTER-THOUGHT

The three of us, friends for more than 60 years in 1997, sat in the cockpit of "Wild Turkey," a 40-foot sloop we had several days earlier sailed out of Road Harbor at Tortola in the British Virgin Islands. It was very early evening and we were moored in the fading November daylight on Manchioneel Bay off Cooper Island. We had settled down for a couple of drinks - Barbados rum, tonic and lime - before taking the dinghy ashore for dinner.

"To Jerry," Bob Tully said, raising his glass toward Ned Inglish and then in my direction. We matched thc gesture in memory of a friend, Jerry Metcalf, who had died almost two years earlier of a substantial coronary, and who had enlisted and served with us in the United States Marine Corps when we were 17 and barely out of a St. Louis high school.

The toast had accompanied the first drink of each evening since Bob and I had arrived on St. Thomas in the U.S. Virgins, where Ned had lived for the past six months. Our trip centered around this short voyage aboard "Wild Turkey," made possible by Bob's sailing experience, particularly in this pan of the Carribean, and Ned's presence in the Islands. It was a reunion based on the pessimistic and unspoken assumption that when you reach your late 60s there's a receding chance you'll be around to do it again.

As we sat in the failing light, soothed by a combination of tropical air and rum, we reminisced about our distant school days during The Great Depression. That was the economic depression of the 1930s, named, I suppose, to distinguish it from The Not So Great Depression, which must have been a real bummer.

We also talked about our Marine Corps experiences, which with the exception of Ned and another absent friend who had enlisted with us were neatly tucked between the Second World War and the Korean business in the early 1950s. That fortunate bit of timing may have allowed Bob and me to reach relative old age. On the other hand, Ned and the absent friend, Ed Kelly, needed more luck because they had enlisted in the Marine reserves after our military discharges in 1948 and both were recalled for service in Korea two years later.

Ned admits his enlistment in the reserves had more to do with the monthly check he got to supplement his college expenses than with any deeply felt need to do close order drill. Ed, retired and living in St. Louis, where Ned still maintained his permanent residence, never disclosed to me his reasons for joining the reserves. But, then, I'd only seen Ed several times since 1948 when the two of us took our discharge pay to New York and spent it in the old jazz bars on 52nd Street and on tickets to see "A Streetcar Named Desire" when that Tennessee Williams play was new and its cast contained a young Marlon Brando and other actors who also subsequently achieved successful film careers. The ones I recall are Jessica Tandy, Karl Malden and Kim Hunter.

The first few days after our reunion on St. Thomas were spent with mornings on the beach at Magens Bay, a popular destination for tourists from the resort hotels as well as others off the glitzy cruise ships that visit the island with the regularity of the prevailing winds that cooled Ned's residence. In a phone conversation with me before I'd left my home in Michigan, Ned had described his quarters as a " basement apartment" with a view of several offshore islands. I had trouble visualizing a basement with a view until I saw his place, which was the first floor of a two-story building atop a mountain reachable by a barely paved switchback road more treacherous than Benedict Arnold. But the prevailing breeze, commanding view and absolute seclusion made the ascent worth the effort and the hazard.

We made that ascent several times a day, going to and returning from the beach and long, leisurely dinners where I learned things about my old friends I had not known. Tully, I discovered, could make a Grand Marnier soufflé and rebuild thc carburetor on a 1976 Ford Falcon convertible, one of which he had garaged at his home in Dallas. He could also make Coq au Vin, Coquilles St. Jacques and God knows what else despite a childhood in which a cheeseburger was associated with fine dining. And he could skipper a moderately large sailboat with more than ordinary skill.

I also learned after more than 60 years of friendship that the eccentric spelling of Ned Inglish's family name derived from the War of 1812. One of Ned's ancestors fought in that war on the American side and changed the spelling from "English" to "Inglish" out of contempt for the British. That only proves that an obscure symbolic act, if strongly felt, can endure as long as the famous ones.

Bob and I had come to the Virgin Islands to sail, but Ned had come the previous May to invest in and fly a twin-engine, 10 passenger airplane. Although he had been in the commercial baking business for 40 years, Ned is a veteran pilot with some 3,000 flying hours and has had a variety of licenses that allowed him to do most things any flier would want to do with a machine that defies gravity.

In the six months he'd been in the Islands, he had mainly had to concern himself with keeping his expensive airplane from being blown into the next hemisphere by a series of hurricanes and tropical storms that threatened and wrecked havoc on the region. He seemed constantly on the verge of flying the plane out to some safe haven, usually another island out of the current storm's path.

The storms that plagued Ned's life came a year after Hurricane Marilyn ripped the island apart. That particular force of nature crippled most of St. Thomas' hotel and tourist facilities, and left many of the private houses roofless. A good percentage of those roofs had been only partially repaired with some blue sub-surface construction material that gave the green mountain sides a blue-speckled appearance. The half finished work, Ned thought, was consistent with the casual island approach to most projects, construction or otherwise.

On the third day, we took the ferry from Red Hook on St. Thomas in the U.S. Virgins to Soper's Hole on Tortola in the British islands. The trip took less than an hour and we rode over on the top deck, open to a mainly clear but hazy sky. It was either hazy or I was up too early after another night of drinks, dinner at the shoreline and more drinks. But anything worth doing, I've always felt, is worth doing to excess.

After we had cleared British customs, we took a van from Soper's Hole to the Roadtown marina where our boat was based. The driver assured us the trip would take 19 ½ minutes, a claim I didn't bother to verify because it sounded like a line he used on all his passengers. As a matter of strongly held conviction, I demand originality from van drivers.

At the marina, we were put through an orientation with others to familiarize us with the boats and a good deal of additional information designed to keep us from wrecking those expensive vessels. Bob appeared to understand all this detail while Ned and I maintained impenetrable expressions meant to disguise our fundamental ignorance. As it turned out, Bob - who had sailed these waters a number of times -seemed to be the most experienced of the skippers in our orientation group.

Once that boat school was out, we got provisions from a nearby store and stowed the goods aboard "Wild Turkey," which was docked next to a similar sloop occupied by two couples who were also preparing to sail out of Road Harbor. They seemed like a fun-loving bunch, but who doesn't when they're about to cruise the Caribbean for no other purpose than pleasure. The two men were friendly but busy with their boat and the women, particularly one of them, were just friendly. They were probably in their mid to late 30s and were from the U.S. south, a fact easily discernible from their accents even before one of the men disclosed that he and his companion had grown up together on the Gulf coast.

We conducted an intermittent conversation with them as Bob made sure everything was in order, and then we cast off and began to motor slowly away from the dock.

The friendliest of the two women - her long, shapely legs showing the whole marina off to good advantage - elected to dispatch us. She was probably thinking these three old farts won't make it out of the harbor, but she graciously expressed another thought. "Three drunken sailors," she said, waving goodbye.

It was early afternoon before we were underway, sailing on long tacks from one side of the Sir Francis Drake Channel to the other. We were headed for Trellis Bay off Beef Island, which was connected to Tortola by bridge but made a decent afternoon sail. Bob, who was at the helm, used the time to begin our instruction in seamanship. He put us to work hoisting sails once we had cleared the harbor, and he explained the functions of various lines, winches, cleats and other miscellaneous boat stuff.

Ned and I had a lot to learn but the pace was leisurely and we knew there would be a "To Jerry" at the end of the day. The thought reminded me of Metcalf who had attended the University of Missouri at Columbia with me in the days before state schools had built separate campuses in every village and hamlet with a vacant pasture. After our Marine Corps discharges, Ned had gone to a small college in western Missouri and Bob trundled off to a university in Illinois not to be confused with the University of Illinois. It wasn't the Ivy League, but we were just three guys out of The Depression.

I recalled that Jerry had wrecked his car - an old Dodge coupe - late one night outside Columbia and was lying semi-conscious on the roadside when a state trooper arrived to investigate the accident. Although Jerry's car was demolished, he had sustained only a few odd bruises and had fully regained his senses when the officer asked him his name. "Sam Smith, Jerry Metcalf replied.

I can only assume the trooper chalked the response up to trauma because Jerry wasn't arrested for smart-mouthing an officer. But the anecdote, as I told it that evening as we had the first rum and tonics of the trip, evoked, at least for me, some basic element of our dead friend's personality. He was an unreconstructed smart-ass.

We went ashore that first night for dinner at The Last Resort, where they served a buffet with roast beef and Yorkshire pudding. We were, after all, in the British Virgin Islands. The place was well attended by other sailors, whose boats were moored in the bay with "Wild Turkey." The dining room was also attended by two dogs of heavily mixed ancestry who were apparently on their home turf. We had seen them earlier that evening when a young man in a dinghy had motored up to our boat to collect the mooring fee. The dogs had been with him, and they were as much at home in that dinghy as they were in the dining room at The Last Resort.

We had separate double berths aboard "Wild Turkey," which was designed to accommodate six people in crowded efficiency. I awoke the first night out in the middle of a patently Freudian dream to discover water gently pelting me in the face. It was several minutes before I realized that the hatch directly above my head was open and it was raining. It was only later that I connected the dream with the precipitation.

The next morning we had our first breakfast at sea in the cockpit where we could enjoy the fine morning and lie to one another about how good we felt despite the drinks we'd had the previous night. For variety, we changed the morning meal from cornflakes and bananas, which we had eaten every day on St. Thomas, to plain cornflakes.

Some time after nine that morning we left Trellis Bay and set a course for Virgin Gorda, a neighboring island named because its horny discoverer saw a land mass that reminded him of a large woman lying on her back. I wondered if someone in the crew had left the overhead hatch open during an overnight rain.

The weather was good that day in the Drake Channel as we continued what was becoming a voyage of discovery. We were discovering things about our past we had not known or had forgotten over the years. We recalled, among other things, the names of the elementary school teachers who had struggled to educate us. There was Miss Wack and Miss Burnett along with Miss Quinn and, our unanimous favorites, Miss Farrell and Miss O'Tool. The Misses Farrell and O'Tool, in those days when women were not allowed to marry and to teach in the public school system, had somehow managed to combine the command qualities of a five-star general with genuine concern for the young knuckleheads they optimistically tried to inform.

The recollection of those teachers led to further recollections of certain students and events. I could almost smell the cloakrooms - which was the nomenclature for coatrooms in those days - where the aroma of damp wool filled the steam-heated air on snowy winter days.

I recalled one of our classmates, a skinny kid named Paul Pierce who sat in the back of Miss Burnett's fifth grade class and sang dirty songs for those of us close enough to hear him. I must have been about 10 years old then, and I was 68 as I remembered one of the lyrics as we held a steady course for Virgin Gorda.

There's a skeeter on my peter, oh Maree

There's another on my brother, can't you see?

There must be dozens on my cousins

Can't you hear those bastards buzzin'?

There's a skeeter on my peter, oh Maree.

I remember that snippet of pre-pubescent obscenity, but I had no recollection of the singer before or beyond the fifth grade. It was as though Paul Pierce had been divinely installed in that one class at a specific time to sing a dumb song I'd recall 58 years later. The mind is a curious instrument.

There was good wind that day and we took turns, under Bob's supervision, at the helm of 'Wild Turkey," which was a customized Beneteau Oceanis 400 with an overall length of 39 feet, three inches and a 13 foot beam. It had a draft of six feet, six inches and a 50 horsepower diesel engine. The boat carried almost 40 gallons of fuel, more than 130 gallons of water and it had two heads and three showers, counting the one near the dive platform behind the cockpit. It also carried a lot of ice because man doesn't live by bread alone.

We moored in Gorda Sound that afternoon, and took the dinghy ashore to scout The Bitter End, a restaurant where we planned to have dinner that evening. We had not come far that day as the crow flies but it had been another good sail as the boat tacks, and we were ready to settle down with a rum and tonic at a table overlooking the water. In deference to an emerging tradition, we withheld the "To Jerry" until our return to Wild Turkey" for cocktail hour.

After we had gone back to the boat, showered and met our cocktail obligations, we returned to The Bitter End for pre-dinner drinks on a broad terrace adjacent to the restaurant. We got into a conversation with a couple at a table near ours, and learned they were residents of a suburban Detroit community only a few miles from the one where I live. The husband had retired from General Motors and they now split their time between Michigan and the British Virgins, where they had a house and a boat. "It's a small world," I told them, knowing better.

We had our choice that night between one of the restaurant dinners or something the menu identified as the "dinner-buffet." We chose the dinner-buffet, which gave us enough food to provision three cavalry regiments. This was the fourth consecutive night we'd had large meals, and I was beginning to feel like one of those force-fed geese who produce the livers for pate de fois gras.

The next morning was a carbon copy of the previous one, down to the cornflakes and the recollection of overnight rain in my face. The great weather and the company of friends as we had coffee in the cockpit was more than enough to vanquish what at home would have been a hangover.

The winds early that day were irregular and it took longer than usual, Bob told us, to clear the area near Gorda Sound and get on a long tack back down the Drake Channel toward Cooper Island where we would spend our last night on 'Wild Turkey." A cold beer in his hand, Bob leaned back and held the wheel steady with his feet.

Tully and I were both divorced from women named Ann, and the similarity of our circumstances doesn't end there. We continued to have amicable relationships with those women to the extent my ex-wife only lives a few miles from me and Bob's at that time was even closer. His wife, following their divorce, moved from their home in Dallas to New York where they had lived in the 1960s when they were first married. Bob got an apartment after the divorce but subsequently moved back into the house, which was still jointly owned, and he was living there when his ex-wife returned to Texas and moved in with him.

Bob, who liked the arrangement at the time but eventually came to understand why they'd ended the marriage, explained that his ex-wife's return to the Dallas house ended a relationship he had with another woman. "She didn't think I should be living with my ex-wife," Tully told us, "and I certainly understood her position." Divorce, I thought, can sometimes make strange bedfellows.

Neither Bob nor I became parents, but Ned has two grown children and a legal wife to boot. Not literally, of course. That wife, Marlene, apparently didn't share his enthusiasm for the Virgin Islands and at that time had not spent more than a few days at a time there. She preferred to run the family bakery in St. Louis, where their married daughter had joined her with the intention of one day managing the business. Their son, an attorney, also lived in St. Louis but later moved to Denver.

As the wind began to pick up and Great Bog Island appeared on our starboard side, Ned said his son as a small boy had one of those peculiar preferences that often show up in children. "Every time we had breakfast in a restaurant," Ned recalled, "the kid wanted steak."

His parents would always divert him to pancakes or some other more conventional fare, but that only distracted him for the moment. The point of Ned's story derived from a vacation his son took with his maternal grandparents. The four-year-old as usual asked for steak at breakfast one morning and his grandfather let him have it. "To this day almost 30 years later," Ned said, "the boy remembers that steak and loves his grandfather's memory for it"

As usual, we radioed the restaurant on Cooper Island for dinner reservations once we had moored on Manchioneel Bay. But the resort there had a large group of travel agents in for freebies and we couldn't get a table until eight thirty, which was a shade late given the time we began our cocktail hour. We got an early start because it was the eve of the 221st Marine Corps birthday, surely as good an excuse as any for an additional drink.

We weren't drunk, but we were probably a little noisier than usual as the hostess led us to a table on the second level of a terraced dining area overlooking the bay. I noticed that several diners at adjacent tables looked at us with mild distain, an attitude converted to strong disapproval when one of us accidentally knocked a flowerpot off a low ledge. The pot shattered on the level below us, narrowly missing a table occupied by what we later learned were Finnish lesbian sailors. I remark their nationality, sexual preference and maritime inclination only because those three terms, used together, are so definitive.

Although our entrance didn't bode well for the evening, things improved rapidly and we had a fine Caribbean meal as well as a series of genuinely friendly encounters with some of the travel agents and others who were willing to gamble small parts of their evening on a trio of voluble geezers. The travel agents, mostly women, were very different from an impression I'd formed of them years before. I was told by a woman airline employee I once knew that travel agents on complimentary trips or junkets were magnetized by cooked shrimp. She said all you had to do was put out a shrimp bowl at a cocktail party and travel agents would be instantly drawn to it. These travel agents, as far as I could tell, seemed shrimp resistant.

I had a long conversation over after dinner drinks at the outdoor bar with a bright, young Jamaican woman who worked in that island's tourist industry. She was living in New York but told me she missed her home. She talked about the violence in the City, ignoring the violence that has afflicted Jamaica from time to time. The difference for her may have been the distinction between the familiar and the unfamiliar, but a blunt trauma to the head has pretty much the same effect wherever you get it.

I slept well the last night aboard "Wild Turkey," the result, no doubt, of the number of drinks I'd had earlier and the gracious absence of rain pouring onto my face through that infernal overhead hatch. We assembled our gear early the next morning, had another leisurely breakfast under the cockpit canopy - which Bob had rigged to provide shade - and then motored back to Road Harbor where we turned the boat in at the marina.

The same van driver we'd had several days earlier drove us from Roadtown back to Sopor's Hole to catch the ferry to St. Thomas. It was Sunday and the boat was crowded with islanders, many of them in dress clothes, coming and going I knew not where. The return to St. Thomas took about twice as long as the trip over because we had an unscheduled - as far as we knew - stop on St. John island to deal with U.S. customs. The trip would have been entirely uneventful had the ferry pilot not backed the boat into the dock between two other nearby vessels of similar size with considerable skill and perhaps a little more confidence than the space deemed prudent. "Holy shit," someone commented as we glided gently past one of the boats, missing it by inches. I may have been the commentator.

That night on St. Thomas we had dinner with a person Ned described as his "landlady," an attractive woman originally from Guadeloupe in the French West Indies and something of a local television celebrity as the result of an issues-oriented program she hosted at the local public broadcasting station. She had a great deal of charm as well as a sense of time we northerners usually associate with the southern hemisphere. The woman was supposed to meet us at eight and it was well after nine when she appeared, unaware that gross tardiness in some places is a near capital offense.

We had a very good meal at a place called Cafesito, a restaurant in what I presumed is downtown St. Thomas. By the time we got there, few diners were in evidence but the hostess who greeted us was reluctant to provide the large table we requested and could plainly tell was not likely to be put to any other use. It apparently offended her sense of symmetry to give four people a table that could accommodate six. But Ned's landlady dealt with her reluctance with both efficiency and grace. "Let me speak to the manager," she said, and a few minutes later we had the larger table. I then realized her sense of time may be lodged in the southern hemisphere, but her ability to handle an adversary was pure northern corporate raider. I suspected she was one tough cookie despite the gentle smile and manner.

The next morning we were back at Magens Bay and the beach restaurant where we each had three eggs, bacon and a pile of fried potatoes that were guaranteed to clog every artery in a large body. But we justified the indulgence on the grounds we were otherwise faced with cornflake overdose.

After a morning on the beach spent swimming, walking in the sand and surf, lounging and beer-drinking, we returned to the food concession, which was filled by that time with honeymooners and other miscellaneous tourists. We were sitting at one of the outdoor tables with the remnants of our lunches when a reasonably young but dissolute-looking man in a nearby chair struck up an unsolicited conversation with us. His lunch, I noticed, consisted of a vast pile of French fries, which he continued to eat as he began what turned out to be a monologue.

He was at the beach, he said, to search with a metal detector for lost articles of value, an effort made modestly profitable by the hordes of tourists that passed over those sands each day. He either sold the articles back to the original owners or disposed of his findings for cash in other ways he didn't disclose. This little treasure hunt, it turned out, was only a supplement to his regular work as a salvage diver.

We made the mistake of showing interest in that work, which led him to confide that his wife had recently left him and taken their newborn son with her. He confirmed this revelation by showing us a snapshot of an attractive blonde woman, and confessing that he probably drank too much. He said he planned to seek help for the problem, but I had the impression he was more interested in treasure than in professional counsel.

The man had a compulsion toward public disclosure unseen outside the U.S. Securities and Exchange

Commission. But he finally purged himself of those rats, bats and toads inside his head, and left us conversationally spent at Magens Bay. We managed to recover by evening when we went out for our final reunion dinner before Bob and I left for our respective homes the next day.

We ate at one of the major resorts, which was newly remodeled, repaired and reopened a year after Hurricane Marilyn had come to visit. The spacious dining room, exposed on three sides to the salubrious night air, was sparsely occupied, probably because we were ahead of the high tourist season.

We'd had a couple of drinks at Ned's apartment and were having another round at our table when the waiter delivered a basket of dinner rolls. A master baker, Ned had the habit of smelling the bottom of bread, which told him, he told us, if it was rancid or not. As the result of this practice, his children had long since refused to eat with him in any public place.

Bob and I had become accustomed over the past week to Ned's bread-sniffing, but we were surprised that evening when he smelled the bread and called the waiter back to our tableside. "This is crap," he said, demanding to see the baker or pastry chef or someone responsible for what he knew was half-baked and originally frozen. Bob and I, meanwhile, were rocked with laughter, realizing that Ned had tolerated what he considered baking incompetence all week and could stand it no longer. We all have our breaking points and he'd reached his.

Ned is a big man and can assume a stern presence, but I think there was little fear among the wait staff, mainly because his companions had been reduced to near hysterical laughter. Never-the-less, the waiter summoned a sweet-talking young woman from the kitchen who, I suspected, was covering for a cowardly boss. She listened carefully to Ned's baking instructions, removed the offending bread, and returned some time later with a batch that settled the matter. The rolls, I'm sure, were still not up to Ned's standards, but he'd made his point and that, I gathered, was the point.

We awoke the next morning to a deluge, which had begun while we slept. Water was seeping under the glass doorwall that separated Ned's living room from a recently enlarged terrace, and the offshore islands, normally visible from there, had disappeared behind heavy, dark cloudbanks. As Bob and I packed our bags and Ned mopped the increasing flow of water near the door, I realized the timing of the rain - coming as it did at the end of the trip - was near perfect. The timing would edge even closer to perfection a little later when the rain stopped just before we left for the airport.

The True End of the Whole Damn Thing